SEMPRE
Avanti!
WORKBOOK 1

A FUN-FILLED COMPREHENSIVE ITALIAN COURSE
MICHAEL SEDUNARY/ELIO GUARNUCCIO
CIS EDUCATIONAL
RADIO PROGRAMS BY ABC EDUCATION

CIS Educational

Cardigan Street Publishers
an imprint of CIS•Cardigan Street
245 Cardigan Street
Carlton Victoria Australia 3053
Telephone (03) 9349 1211
Facsimile (03) 9347 0175

First published in 1986
Reprinted 1986, 1987, 1989, 1991, 1992 (twice), 1993, 1995, 1996

Designed by Mimmo Cozzolino with the assistance of
Rosanna Di Risio, Shane Nagle, Megan Stone, Any Excuse,
Elio Guarnuccio and Michael Sedunary
Illustrated by Neil Curtis
Additional illustrations by Gaston Vanzet
Radio producer: Elizabeth Woods
Proofreading: Walter Musolino, Sue Romanin
We wish to thank Datapro for the use of their computers
in the preparation of the crossword puzzles
Thanks also to Doris Fiorentini for the collection of realia in Italy

Typeset in Trade Gothic by Leader Composition Pty Ltd
Printed in Australia by Griffin Paperbacks, Adelaide

National Library of Australia Cataloguing-in-Publication data

Guarnuccio, Elio.
  Sempre avanti! workbook 1.

  For children and adults.
  ISBN 0 949919 06 3.

  1. Italian language – Composition and exercises.
  I. Sedunary, Michael. II. Title.

PROFILO PERSONALE

QUEST'INFORMAZIONE È CONFIDENZIALE.

NOME _____

COGNOME _____

INDIRIZZO _____

CLASSE _____

SCUOLA _____

DATA DI NASCITA _____

LUOGO DI NASCITA _____

SEGNO ZODIACALE _____

ETÀ _____

FAMIGLIA _____ **SORELLE** _____ **FRATELLI** _____

NAZIONALITÀ _____

ALTEZZA _____

PESO _____

COLORE PREFERITO _____

SPORT PREFERITO _____

TIFO PER _____

CANTANTE PREFERITO _____

PIATTO PREFERITO _____

FRUTTA PREFERITA _____

PASSATEMPO PREFERITO _____

MATERIA PREFERITA _italiano_____

ANIMALE PREFERITO _____

SPIAGGIA PREFERITA _____

REGIONE D'ITALIA PREFERITA _____

UNA MIA FOTO RECENTE

You may not be able to fill in all of the information at the start,
but you can complete it as you learn the appropriate vocabulary.

CONTENTS

You're wasting your time and money. It's cheaper to buy a copy of this book than to photocopy it!

INTRODUCTION

○ For each chapter in the **Sempre Avanti!** textbook there is a corresponding chapter of exercises and activities in the workbooks:

Chapters 1-10 in Workbook I,
Chapters 11-20 in Workbook 2.

○ An attempt has been made to graduate exercises according to degree of difficulty (as explained in the textbook introduction) but teachers will find that they will need to exercise their discretion in deciding the exact order in which they will be done. Rather than proceed relentlessly from exercise A to exercise Z, teachers may want to combine a grammar exercise with a crossword, for example, and then do a cultural activity from the **Italia Oggi** section. At times it may be better not to exhaust in one sitting similar exercises on a given point but to save some for revision at some later date. Individual teachers will devise their own ways of using the workbooks selectively and creatively.

○ **Parliamo.** Although these exercises are found in the textbook we offer a reminder that most students will find some written preparation for these very useful.

○ **Domande sul fumetto.** These have probably been answered orally already, but space is provided in the workbooks for written answers as well.

○ **Ascoltiamo.** The audio material for these exercises is on the Sempre Avanti! cassettes - but not within the broadcast radio section.

○ **Scriviamo.** Most of the workbooks are devoted to written exercises which give practice in points of grammar illlustrated in the text. Points that are dealt with in summary fashion in the textbook are explained in more complete detail before students are required to attempt any exercises.

In this course students are encouraged to maintain an active, perceptive attitude towards the workings of the Italian language. They are regularly asked in the workbooks to notice how language is used in the text and write down their conclusions about the rules of grammar. The teacher will have a role in helping to formulate these conclusions.

○ **Componimento.** The grammar and vocabulary exercises are not ends in themselves: they are intended to equip students with the language skills that they need to compose Italian of their own.

An attempt has been made to provide scope for a variety of writing modes and to relate topics to situations encountered in the text.

Students could also use the points under the heading of **Conversiamo** in the textbook as the basis for writing dialogues of their own.

○ **L'Italia Oggi.** In this section the students' reading comprehension skills will often be fully extended. The use of ''realia'' such as magazine clippings, maps and travel brochures will acquaint them with the written language of modern life in Italy.

○ Throughout the workbooks the symbol ☑ is used to give the example (modello).

Buon lavoro!
Michael Sedunary and Elio Guarnuccio.

CAPITOLO UNO
ALL'AEROPORTO

ASCOLTIAMO

A. Listen to the greetings people give and circle the one you hear: ⭐

	Arrivederci	Buonanotte	Ciao	Buongiorno	Salve
🙂	Arrivederci	Buonanotte	Ciao	(Buongiorno)	Salve
1.	Arrivederci	Buonanotte	Ciao	Buongiorno	Salve
2.	Arrivederci	Buonanotte	Ciao	Buongiorno	Salve
3.	Arrivederci	Buonanotte	Ciao	Buongiorno	Salve
4.	Arrivederci	Buonanotte	Ciao	Buongiorno	Salve
5.	Arrivederci	Buonanotte	Ciao	Buongiorno	Salve
6.	Arrivederci	Buonanotte	Ciao	Buongiorno	Salve
7.	Arrivederci	Buonanotte	Ciao	Buongiorno	Salve
8.	Arrivederci	Buonanotte	Ciao	Buongiorno	Salve
9.	Arrivederci	Buonanotte	Ciao	Buongiorno	Salve
10.	Arrivederci	Buonanotte	Ciao	Buongiorno	Salve

B. Now circle the expression people use to say how they feel: ⭐ ⭐

	Non c'è male	Malissimo	Male	Benone	Benino
🙂	Non c'è male	Malissimo	Male	Benone	(Benino)
1.	Non c'è male	Malissimo	Male	Benone	Benino
2.	Non c'è male	Malissimo	Male	Benone	Benino
3.	Non c'è male	Malissimo	Male	Benone	Benino
4.	Non c'è male	Malissimo	Male	Benone	Benino
5.	Non c'è male	Malissimo	Male	Benone	Benino
6.	Non c'è male	Malissimo	Male	Benone	Benino
7.	Non c'è male	Malissimo	Male	Benone	Benino
8.	Non c'è male	Malissimo	Male	Benone	Benino
9.	Non c'è male	Malissimo	Male	Benone	Benino
10.	Non c'è male	Malissimo	Male	Benone	Benino

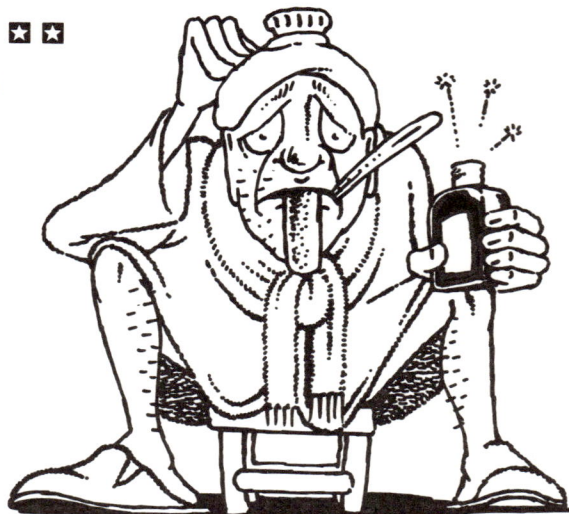

SCRIVIAMO

A. Domande sul fumetto.
   Answer the following questions based on the cartoon strip in Italian. Begin your sentence with either _sì_ or _no_. ★

   ☑ Angela è una bambina? _No, non è una bambina._

   ☑ La mamma di Angela è antiquata? _Sì, è antiquata._

   1. Angela ha tutto?_____

   2. Lo zaino è pieno?_____

   3. Angela ha il pullover giallo?_____

   4. Dario è più alto?_____

   5. Ha un orecchino?_____

   6. È magro?_____

   7. È un po' nervoso?_____

   8. Giorgio è forte?_____

   9. È simpatico quando ha lo stomaco vuoto?_____

   10. Kevin ha la roba in uno zaino?_____

B. Essere.

Essere	to be
sono	I am
sei	you are (sing.)
è	he, she, it is
siamo	we are
siete	you are (pl.)
sono	they are

> Essere o non essere

   Complete the following using the appropriate form of _essere_. ★

   ☑ Sì, ho tutto, ___Sono___ sicura.

   1. Ma, Angelina cara, _____ sicura che hai tutto?

   2. Mammaa!! _____ veramente antipatica.

   3. Dario ha un orecchino! _____ più alto, _____ più magro.

   4. Mamma, _____ così antiquata. Dario _____ simpatico e non _____ molto magro.

   5. Uffa, questa valigia _____ veramente pesante!

   6. Presto, mamma, abbiamo solo venti minuti; _____ in ritardo.

   7. Angela, Dario e Giorgio _____ all'aeroporto oggi.

   8. Presto, ragazzi, _____ pronti per la partenza?

   9. Scusa Angela, dov' _____ l'edicola?

   10. Angela e Dario, perchè _____ sempre in ritardo?

C. Avere.

Avere	to have
ho	I have
hai	you have (sing.)
ha	he, she, it has
abbiamo	we have
avete	you have (pl.)
hanno	they have

Complete the following using the appropriate form of <u>avere</u>. ★

☑ Presto, mamma, *abbiamo* solo venti minuti.

1. Ma, Angelina cara, sei sicura che _____ tutto?

2. Sì, _____ tutto, sono sicura.

3. Sì, Dario è differente; è più alto e _____ un orecchino.

4. Non sono pigro. Tu non _____ una valigia così pesante.

5. Quando _____ lo stomaco vuoto sono antipatico.

6. Giorgio, Kevin ed io _____ tutta la roba in questa valigia piccola.

7. Attenzione! L'aereo è quasi pronto per la partenza; _____ solo venti minuti.

8. Kevin e Angela non _____ molto tempo.

D. Complete the following using the appropriate form of <u>essere</u>. ★

☑ Giorgio, sta' zitto! Macchè, non _sei_ forte?

1. Sono forte, sì, ma _____ anche stanco.

2. Giorgio, _____ così pigro!

3. È la valigia. _____ pesantissima!

4. _____ a Tullamarine, l'aeroporto di Melbourne.

5. Uei, ragazzi, l'aereo è pronto per la partenza; _____ in ritardo.

6. Tutti i ragazzi _____ pronti adesso.

7. Giorgio non _____ simpatico quando ha lo stomaco vuoto.

8. Kevin, _____ così bravo, così intelligente.

E. Complete the following using the appropriate form of <u>avere</u>. ★

☑ Non c'è il pullover giallo ma _ho_ il golfino rosso.

1. Angela non ha una valigia, _____ uno zaino.

2. A Roma Angela _____ bisogno di un vestito di moda.

3. Dario, _____ una rivista per il volo?

4. Ma Giorgio, perchè _____ una valigia piena di pasta?

5. Io _____ tutta la roba in questa valigia. È forte, no?

6. Kevin e Giorgio non _____ un orecchino.

F. Nouns – singular endings.

masculine	-o	-e
feminine	-a	-e

Nouns in Italian are either *masculine* or *feminine* in gender. This applies to things as well as people. For example **vestito** is a *masculine noun*, **valigia** is *feminine*. Of course, sex has nothing to do with it. There is nothing particularly masculine about a dress or feminine about a suitcase.

> *Masculine* and *feminine* are part of the terminology of language learning which you will come to know. Like all technical language, the terminology of grammar is used to make things easier, not more difficult. Don't let it put you off!!

Most Italian nouns ending in **-o** are *masculine.*
Most Italian nouns ending in **-a** are *feminine.*
Nouns ending in **-e** may be either *masculine* or *feminine.*
You have to learn the gender of **-e** words as you learn their meaning. There are a few words, like **gioventù,** that don't fit the above pattern. You will learn them as you encounter them.

Write (m) or (f) in the brackets next to the following words: ⭐

1. ragazzo ( )	6. stomaco ( )	11. sedia ( )	16. valigia ( )
2. ragazza ( )	7. volo ( )	12. edicola ( )	17. classe ( )
3. giornale ( )	8. canzone ( )	13. orecchino ( )	18. riga ( )
4. gioventù ( )	9. lezione ( )	14. signore ( )	19. aereo ( )
5. pasta ( )	10. professore ( )	15. golfino ( )	20. moda ( )

G. Indefinite article.

masculine	un	uno
feminine	una	un'

The term *indefinite article* is used for the words <u>a</u> or <u>an</u>.
e.g. a suitcase, an earring.

The Italian *indefinite articles* are:
before a *masculine* noun, **un**
e.g. **un** vestito, **un** orecchino.
If a *masculine* noun begins with **z** or **s** + *consonant* use **uno**
e.g. **uno** zaino, **uno** spacco.

Before a *feminine* noun, **una**
e.g. **una** valigia, **una** studentessa.
If a *feminine* noun begins with a *vowel,* use **un'**
e.g. **un'**edicola.

Write the correct form of the indefinite article in front of the following: ⭐

🔲 _un_ aereo.

1. _____ aeroporto

2. _____ volo

3. _____ edicola

4. _____ giornale

5. _____ zaino

6. _____ bambina

7. _____ spacco

8. _____ rivista

8. _____ orecchino

10. _____ ragazzo

11. _____ astuccio

12. _____ aula

13. _____ canzone

H. Definite article.

masculine **il l' lo**	
feminine **la l'**	

The term *definite article* is used for the word <u>the</u>.
e.g. <u>the</u> suitcase, <u>the</u> airport, <u>the</u> dress, <u>the</u> earring.
Notice how the pronunciation of the English definite article changes, depending on the first letter of the word that follows.

The Italian *definite articles* are:
before a *masculine* noun **il**
e.g. **il** vestito, **il** giornale.
If a *masculine* noun begins with **z** or **s** + *consonant* use **lo**
e.g. **lo** zaino, **lo** stomaco.
If a *masculine* noun begins with a *vowel* use **l'**
e.g. **l'**aeroporto, **l'**orecchino.

Before a *feminine* noun **la**
e.g. **la** valigia, **la** canzone.
If a *feminine* noun begins with a *vowel* use **l'**
e.g. **l'**edicola.

Write the correct form of the <u>definite article</u> in front of the following: ★

☺ ___*l'*___ aereo   4. _____ edicola   8. _____ gioventù   12. _____ sedia

1. _____ aiuto   5. _____ gabinetto   9. _____ golfino   13. _____ aula

2. _____ bambina   6. _____ giornale   10. _____ spacco   14. _____ valigia

3. _____ canzone   7. _____ giornalaio   11. _____ classe   15. _____ lezione

I. Write the correct <u>indefinite article</u> in front of the following: ★

☺ _*una*_ ragazza   4. _____ edicola   8. _____ giornale   12. _____ professore

1. _____ aereo   5. _____ valigia   9. _____ orecchino   13. _____ porta

2. _____ stomaco   6. _____ golfino   10. _____ zaino   14. _____ banco

3. _____ canzone   7. _____ vestito   11. _____ finestra   15. _____ madre

J. Write the correct <u>definite article</u> in front of the following: ★

☺ _*la*_ moda   4. _____ ragazza   8. _____ canzone   12. _____ gomma

1. _____ orecchino   5. _____ ragazzo   9. _____ giornale   13. _____ gabinetto

2. _____ partenza   6. _____ zaino   10. _____ stomaco   14. _____ signore

3. _____ pasta   7. _____ volo   11. _____ cancellino   15. _____ aeroporto

K. Adjectives (meaning).
Which description of people and things in the cartoon is correct? Write your answer in Italian: ★

☺ Il pullover di Angela è giallo o rosso? *Il pullover di Angela è rosso.*

1. Lo zaino di Angela è pieno o vuoto?_____

2. La mamma di Angela è simpatica o antipatica?_____

3. La gonna di Angela è ridicola o elegante?_____

4. Giorgio è stanco o pigro?_____

5. La valigia di Kevin è pesante o leggera?_____

L. Adjectives (agreement).

> The most important thing to remember about
> *adjectives* is that they *match or agree* with the *person
> or thing* they describe. Use the *masculine form* of the
> adjective with a *masculine noun*, the *feminine form* of
> the adjective with a *feminine noun*.
> e.g. **Lo zaino è pieno ma non è pesante.**
> **La valigia è piena ma non è pesante.**
>
> Some adjectives follow this pattern:
> *masculine* **-o**
> *feminine* **-a**
>
> Others follow this pattern:
> *masculine* **-e**
> *feminine* **-e**

Apply the descriptions used in the following sentences to the person or thing mentioned in brackets underneath.
★ ★

☺ Angela è sicura che ha tutto.

(Giorgio) *Giorgio è sicuro che ha tutto.*

1. Lo zaino è veramente pieno.

(La valigia)_____

2. La mamma di Angela è antipatica.

(Giorgio)_____

3. La gonna di Angela è elegante.

(L'orecchino di Dario)_____

4. Dario è un po' nervoso.

(La mamma di Angela)_____

5. La valigia di Giorgio è pesante.

(Lo zaino di Angela)_____

6. Giorgio è forte, ma è anche stanco.

   (Angela)_____

7. Questa valigia è leggera, comoda e compatta.

   (Questo zaino)_____

8. Kevin è bravo e intelligente.

   (La mamma di Angela)_____

M.Choose from the list of adjectives used in this chapter (see Parole Nuove) to complete the following sentences. Be sure to make adjectives agree with nouns. ★ ★

☺ Sono __forte__, sì, ma sono anche __stanco.__

1. Ma, Angelina cara, sei _____ che hai tutto?

2. Sì, ho tutto. Guarda, questo zaino è veramente _____.

3. Ma Dario, sei così differente! Sei più _____, sei più _____.

4. È un orecchino, signora. È argento _____.

5. Scusa, Angela, dov'è il gabinetto? Sono un po' _____

6. Giorgio, sta'zitto. Sei così _____!

7. Uffa, tu non hai una valigia così _____

8. Quando ho lo stomaco _____ sono _____.

9. Kevin, sei così _____, così _____

10. Tutta la roba in una valigia così _____? _____!!

N. Questo, questa, quest'.
Study the chart in the Riassunto di Grammatica, and formulate some rules for the use of <u>questo</u>. ★

_____

_____

_____

Now write the correct form of <u>questo</u> in front of the following:

☺ __quest'__ orecchino   5. _____ giornalaio   10. _____ ragazza

1. _____ aereo   6. _____ bambina   11. _____ astuccio

2. _____ stomaco   7. _____ rivista   12. _____ lezione

3. _____ edicola   8. _____ vestito   13. _____ aula

4. _____ giornale   9. _____ ragazzo   14. _____ moda

0.

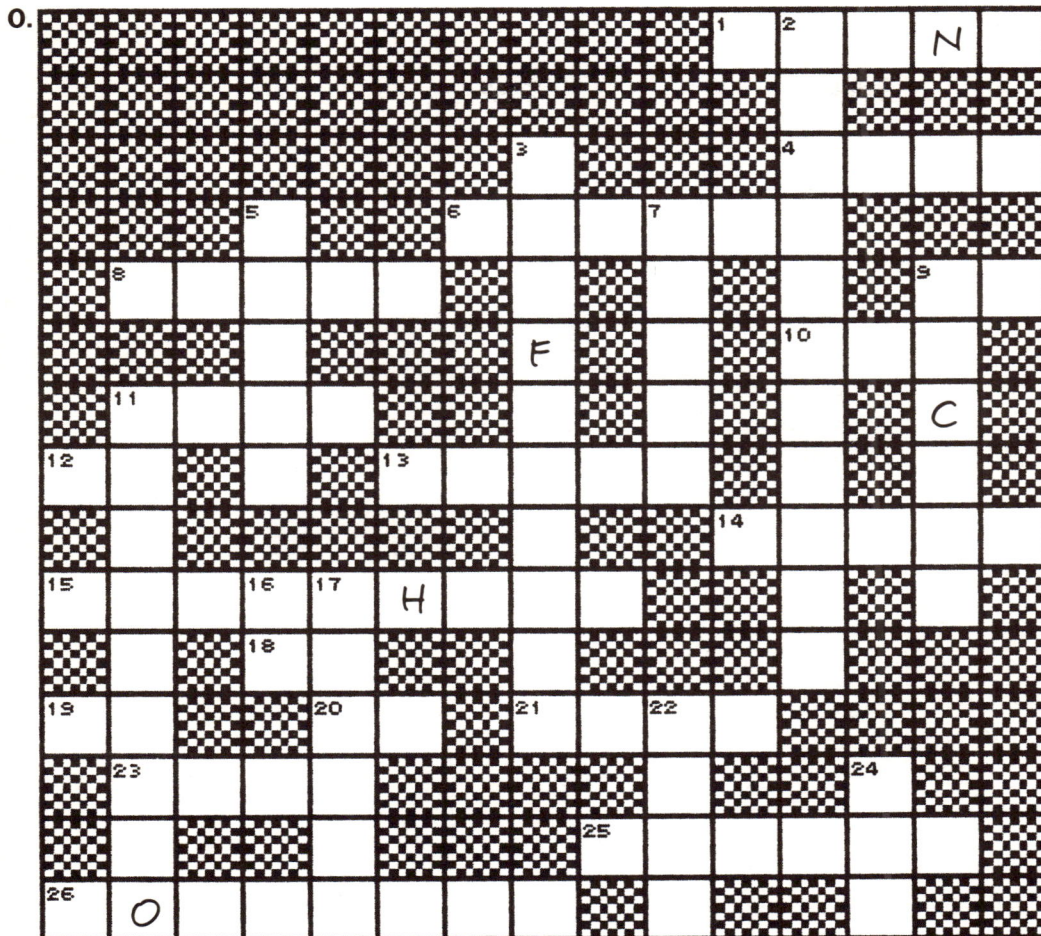

Parole crociate – gli aggettivi. ★

Orizzontali

1. La valigia di Giorgio è . . .
4. L'orecchino è di argento . . .
6. Yellow
8. Giorgio non è contento quando ha lo stomaco . . .
9. If
10. Dario, . . . più alto!
11. Sì, Dario è più . . .
12. A, an
13. Aeroplane
14. Giorgio, sei veramente . . .
15. Cheeky
18. . . . zaino
19. You
20. But
21. Here is!
23. Tall
25. Thank you
26. La valigia di Kevin è . . .

Verticali

2. It's not possible
3. Ma Dario, sei così . . .
5. Strong
7. Not short
9. Hai tutto? Sei . . .
11. Old fashioned
16. . . . giornalaio
17. Questa sedia è molto . . .
22. Dear
24. More

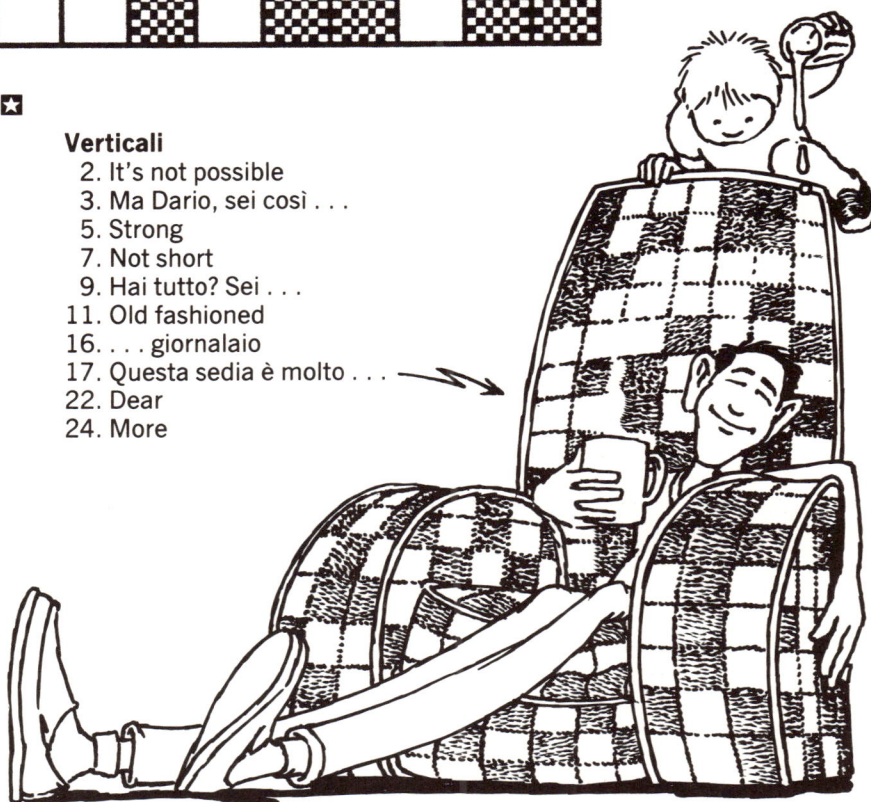

Dario è sempre in ritardo!

P. For each item that is numbered, answer the question: <u>Che cos'è?</u> ⭐ ⭐

1. _____
2. _____
3. _____
4. _____
5. _____
6. _____
7. _____

8. _____
9. _____
10. _____
11. _____
12. _____
13. _____
14. _____

15. _____
16. _____
17. _____
18. _____
19. _____
20. _____
21. _____

Now answer these questions with <u>Sì, c'è,</u> or <u>No, non c'è.</u> ⭐

C'è un libro?_____
C'è un'edicola?_____
C'è una cartella?_____
C'è una sedia?_____
C'é una riga?_____

C'è un quaderno?_____
C'è un professore?_____
C'è un aereo?_____
C'è una gomma?_____
C'è un giornale?_____

C'è una matita?_____
C'è un orecchino?_____
C'è un cancellino?_____
C'è una signorina?_____
C'è una porta?_____

Q. Veramente, troppo, molto, un po', quasi, così. Express the following in Italian: ⭐ ⭐ ⭐

    1. This suitcase is really full._____

    2. The backpack is too heavy._____

    3. Dario is not very thin._____

    4. I'm a bit nervous._____

    5. The plane is nearly ready for departure._____

    6. Dario is really different._____

    7. Giorgio is very lazy._____

    8. Kevin's suitcase is so light, so compact._____

    9. Angela's mum is a bit tired._____

   10. Giorgio's stomach is nearly full._____

R. Write the correct form of _questo_ in front of the following: ⭐

☺ ___questo___ golfino   4. _____ aiuto   8. _____ partenza

1. _____ zaino   5. _____ canzone   9. _____ edicola

2. _____ valigia   6. _____ argento   10. _____ giornale

3. _____ pasta   7. _____ volo   11. _____ classe

S. Absolute superlatives: -issimo, -issima.

> Watch how the **-issimo, -issima** endings can add to the meaning of an ordinary adjective.
>
> **La valigia è pienissima.** The suitcase is absolutely full, completely full, full to the brim.
>
> **Il ragazzo è altissimo.** The boy is extremely tall, very, very tall.
>
> **Lo zaino è pesantissimo.** The backpack is extremely heavy.

Agree emphatically with the following statements: ⭐

☺ Lo zaino è veramente pieno. _Sì, è pienissimo._____

    1. Giorgio è veramente pigro._____

    2. La valigia è così pesante._____

    3. Kevin è molto intelligente._____

    4. Questo zaino è troppo piccolo._____

    5. Dario è nervoso._____

    6. Il vestito è molto elegante._____

    7. Questa ragazza è così simpatica._____

    8. La valigia è molto compatta._____

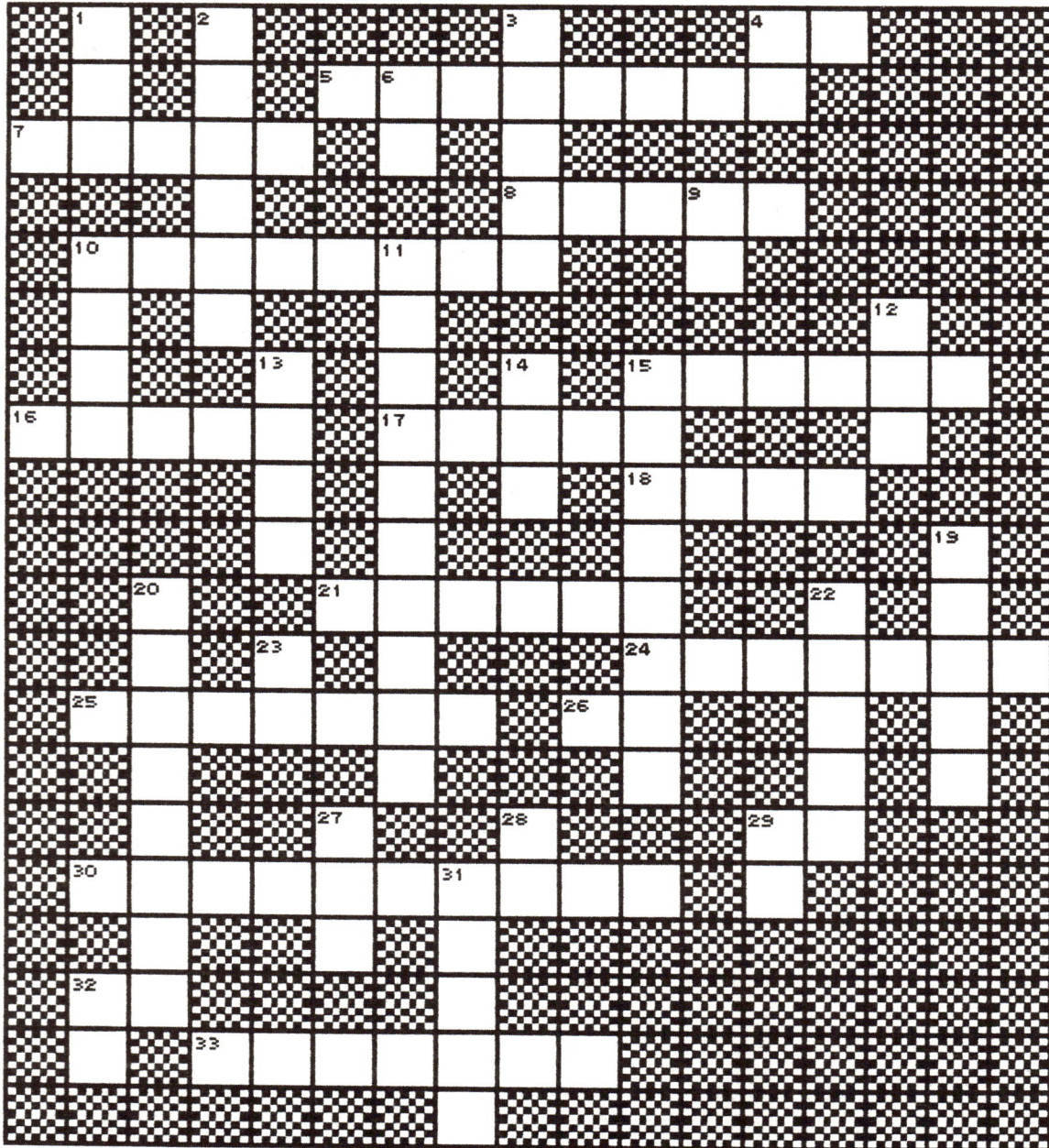

T. Parole crociate – scuola e numeri. ⭐ ⭐

Orizzontali

4. . . . spacco
5. Window
7. Door
8. Chair
10. Pencil case
15. Five
16. Desk
17. Paper
18. Ruler

21. Class
24. Lesson
25. Blackboard
26. . . . ragazzo
29. . . . zaino
30. Male teacher
32. . . . studente
33. Four

Verticali

1. One
2. Pencil
3. Chalk
4. . . . professoressa
6. . . . giornale
9. . . . golfino
10. Classroom
11. Duster
12. Two
13. Nine
14. Three

15. School bag
19. Pen
20. Exercise book
22. Book
23. . . . partenza
27. Six
28. . . . zaino
29. . . . gioventù
31. Seven
32. . . . canzone

U. How did Angela say? ⭐ ⭐

1. Quickly, Mum, we only have twenty minutes._____

2. This backpack is full. Look! It's absolutely full!_____

3. Mum, you're a real pain!_____

4. In Rome I need a fashionable dress._____

5. Dario is nice and he's not very thin._____

6. Giorgio, you're so lazy!_____

7. Oh, Kevin, you are so good, so intelligent!_____

8. Kevin has everything in his tiny little suitcase._____

V. How would you say? ⭐ ⭐ ⭐

1. Quickly, you (pl.) only have twenty minutes._____

2. This suitcase is full. Look! It's absolutely full!_____

_____

3. Mum, you're really nice!_____

4. I need a fashionable jumper._____

5. Dario is a pain, he's very skinny._____

6. Giorgio isn't very lazy._____

7. Kevin is not very intelligent._____

8. I have everything in this convenient backpack._____

_____

W. Parole Nuove. Circle the word you choose: ⭐

1. Which is more for the pupil than for the teacher?
   la lavagna   **il gesso**   **la cartella**   **la gomma**

2. Which won't fit in your <u>astuccio</u>?
   la matita   **la penna**   **la cartella**   **la gomma**

3. Which is the odd number out?
   quattro   **cinque**   **sei**   **otto**   **dieci**

4. Which one won't help keep you warm?
   l'orecchino   **il vestito**   **il golfino**   **la gonna**

5. Which won't you take to read during the flight?
   il libro   **l'edicola**   **il giornale**   **la rivista**

6. Which would you rather be called?
   antipatico   **simpatico**   **pigro**   **ridicolo**

7. Which is the last thing you want your suitcase to be?
   comodo   **compatto**   **pesante**   **leggero**

8. Which expression shows that you're really impressed?
   È forte!   **Che barba!**   **Che disastro!**   **Sei impossibile!**

X. Un po' di tutto. ⭐ ⭐ ⭐
If you can express the following in Italian you can feel confident that you have mastered the material in
Chapter 1. The letter in brackets refers to a Parliamo exercise which you should find helpful.

1. This girl is really disagreeable (a real pain).(A)

_____

2. I'm strong but I'm also nervous. (B)

_____

3. This suitcase is full but the backpack is empty. (C)

_____

4. You're not late, Gina, you have five minutes. (E)

_____

5. This suitcase is really full but it's not too heavy. (F,G)

_____

6. Francesca is very lazy and a bit of a pain. (H)

_____

7. Here is a newspaper but they don't have a magazine. (I,J)

_____

Y. Componimento.

1. **Make up five sentences of your own describing people or objects in your classroom.** ⭐ ⭐ ⭐

   🙂 *Il professore è veramente intelligente.*

   a)_____

   b)_____

   c)_____

   d)_____

   e)_____

2. **Make up a simple little dialogue between your mother and yourself. You're running late for** ⭐ ⭐ ⭐
   school but Mum insists on going through your school bag.

   _____

   _____

   _____

   _____

   _____

   _____

A. Viaggio in Italia. ⭐ ⭐
   Go through pages 23-26 of the textbook
   and mark in on the map below,
   all the places mentioned.

   This map is to be
   used for exercises
   A and C

B. True or False? ⭐ ⭐ ⭐
   Write true or false after the following statements relating to
   the culture unit <u>Viaggio in Italia</u> on pages 23-26 in the textbook.

☑ Angela is keen to photograph major cities and monuments in Italy. _True_

1. Giorgio shares Angela's enthusiasm for monuments._____

2. La Juventus, l'Inter and la Fiorentina are famous Italian restaurants._____

3. The Ponte Vecchio is a famous shop in Florence._____

4. Giorgio has relatives in the north of Italy._____

5. Faye is keen to meet people of her own age in Italy._____

6. Kevin's idea would increase tourism in the city of Pisa._____

7. Capri and Sardegna are both islands popular with tourists._____

8. Mrs. Casati is looking forward to a hectic tour with six energetic youngsters._____

ITALIA con POLVANI

Tour	INIZIO		TERMINE	
215	Aprile	1	Aprile	14
216	Aprile	8	Aprile	21
217	Aprile	15	Aprile	28
218	Aprile	22	Maggio	5
219	Aprile	29	Maggio	12
220	Maggio	6	Maggio	19
221	Maggio	13	Maggio	26
222	Maggio	20	Giugno	2
223	Maggio	27	Giugno	9
224	Giugno	3	Giugno	16
225	Giugno	10	Giugno	23

Durata del viaggio 14 giorni. Pensione completa in alberghi di prima categoria durante tutto il percorso. Mezza pensione a Roma. Camere con bagno privato, negli alberghi indicati o similari.

Il tour può essere iniziato in una qualsiasi delle città previste dal percorso e terminato nella stessa allo scadere dei 14 giorni.

PREZZI PER PERSONA
(camere con bagno privato)

Percorso	Camera doppia	Camera singola
ROMA - ROMA 14 giorni	L. 1.350.000	L. 1.696.000
ROMA - ROMA 12 giorni fino alla colazione del 12° giorno	L. 1.200.000	L. 1.490.000
ROMA - ROMA 8 giorni dalla partenza da Roma del 4° giorno all'arrivo a Roma dell'11° giorno	L. 895.000	L. 1.090.000
Notte extra a Roma (mezza pensione) ROMA	L 80.000	L. 105.000

Roma • Assisi • Firenze • San Gimignano • Siena • Padova • Venezia • Cortina d'Ampezzo • Lago di Garda • Milano • Lugano • Monte-Carlo • Genova • Pisa • Capri • Sorrento • Pompei • Roma

1° giorno (domenica) - ROMA • Riunione in Via Ludovisi 16 - tel. 475.8412 - e trasferimento in hotel. I nostri servizi iniziano con la *cena e l'alloggio.*

2° giorno (lunedi) - ROMA • Giornata intera dedicata alla visita della "città eterna", culla della civiltà occidentale e cuore del Cattolicesimo, oggi centro della vita politica e culturale italiana. La visita include: Musei Vaticani, Cappella Sistina, Piazza San Pietro, Foro Romano, Colosseo, Catacombe, S. Paolo fuori le Mura, S. Pietro in Vincoli con il "Mosè" di Michelangelo. □ *Mezza pensione in hotel.*

3° giorno (martedi) - ROMA • Giornata libera. □ *Mezza pensione in hotel.*

4° giorno (mercoledi) - ROMA • Assistenza alla Benedizione papale e prosecuzione per Firenze passando per Assisi, mistica città medioevale dove San Francesco e Santa Chiara vissero in umiltà e penitenza; visita alla Basilica di San Francesco. □ *Cena e alloggio in hotel a Firenze.*

5° giorno (giovedi) - FIRENZE • Al mattino visita alla città che dette i natali all'immortale poeta Dante Alighieri: storia, arte e vita culturale animano la "città del giglio" e la rendono ineguagliabile. Si visita il Duomo con il Campanile di Giotto, il Battistero, Piazza della Signoria, l'Accademia, Ponte Vecchio, Palazzo Pitti o Cappelle Medicee, Piazzale Michelangelo, dal quale si ammira il panorama rinascimentale della città. □ *Pranzo in un ristorante caratteristico.* Nel pomeriggio escursione a San Gimignano con le sue belle torri medioevali e arrivo a Siena, la città del Palio. Breve visita della città: Piazza del Campo, Torre del Mangia, Cattedrale. Rientro a Firenze in serata. □ *Cena e alloggio in hotel.*

6° giorno (venerdi) - FIRENZE •. Mattinata libera e *pranzo.* Nel pomeriggio partenza per Padova. Sosta per visitare la Basilica di S. Antonio e prosecuzione per Venezia. La singolare posizione sulla laguna, la bellezza dei monumenti che si specchiano nei canali, la ricchezza del patrimonio artistico fanno di Venezia una città unica al mondo. *Cena ed alloggio in hotel.*

□ **7° giorno (sabato) - VENEZIA •** In mattinata visita della città a piedi: Piazza San Marco, Basilica di S. Marco, Palazzo Ducale, Ponte dei Sospiri. Nel pomeriggio partenza per Cortina d'Ampezzo, "regina" delle Dolomiti e una delle località invernali più importanti d'Europa, passando per Vittorio Veneto, la città della vittoria italiana nella prima grande Guerra Mondiale. Situata nel cuore delle Alpi Dolomitiche, a 1.220 metri sul livello del mare, Cortina è un centro di fama internazionale, perfettamente attrezzata per praticare tutti gli sports invernali. □ *Pranzo a Venezia; cena e alloggio in Cortina.*

8° giorno (domenica) - CORTINA • Al mattino partenza per Dobbiaco e Brunico, quindi con l'Autostrada A22 si transita da Bolzano e Trento arrivando a Riva del Garda ove si sosta per il *pranzo.* Continuazione lungo il magnifico litorale del lago di Garda per arrivare a Milano, attraversando Gardone e Salò. Principale centro commerciale e industriale d'Italia, Milano è una grande città moderna che conta secoli di storia ed ha meravigliosi insigni monumenti.
□ *Cena ed alloggio in hotel.*
Tour 217: *Pranzo di Pasqua a Riva del Garda.*

9° giorno (lunedi) - MILANO • Giro panoramico della città. Escursione a Lugano perla del Canton Ticino, in Svizzera, attraversando Como, città della seta, e costeggiando il suo Lago. Arrivo a Lugano, città commerciale, industriale e bancaria, ma soprattutto centro turistico molto conosciuto per il suo clima mite. □ *Pranzo a Lugano; cena ed alloggio in hotel a Milano.*

10° giorno (martedi) - MILANO • Al mattino partenza per Monte-Carlo attraversando l'Autostrada dei Trafori e quella dei Fiori, con vista di Savona, Albenga, San Remo, Ventimiglia, in mezzo a vaste coltivazioni di fiori, si arriva alla frontiera francese. Poi finalmente a Monte-Carlo, centro turistico mondialmente rinomato, gioiello della Costa Azzurra. A Monte-Carlo si potrà ammirare il magnifico panorama del Principato, il Castello del Principe e rendere omaggio alla tomba di Sua Altezza la Principessa Grace. Breve sosta nel famoso Casinò. □ *Pranzo a Monte-Carlo.* Nel pomeriggio prosecuzione per Genova, uno dei più importanti porti del Mediterraneo. □ *Cena ed alloggio in hotel.*

11° giorno (mercoledi) - GENOVA • Al mattino breve giro per la città e partenza per Pisa conosciuta in tutto il mondo per la sua Piazza dei Miracoli e la sua Torre Pendente; città natale di Galileo Galilei. Sosta per visitare la Cattedrale e prosecuzione per Roma percorrendo l'"Autostrada del Sole".
□ *Pranzo durante il cammino; cena ed alloggio in hotel.*

12° giorno (giovedi) - ROMA • Al mattino partenza per Napoli; giro orientativo della città che offre al turista uno spettacolo ineguagliabile per le sue bellezze naturali. Prosecuzione in aliscafo per Capri, isola di sogno per il suo clima mite, il suo mare intensamente azzurro, il suo cielo puro, la sua vegetazione quasi tropicale. Visita alla Grotta Azzurra (se il tempo lo permette). Ritorno a Marina Grande e continuazione per il centro di Capri dove si *pranza.* Nel pomeriggio imbarco sul vaporetto per Sorrento. □ *Cena ed alloggio in hotel.*

13° giorno (venerdi) - SORRENTO • Al mattino partenza per Pompei, l'antica città romana sepolta nel 79 d.C. dalla cenere e dai lapilli eruttati dal Vesuvio. Visita agli Scavi e *pranzo in un ristorante tipico.* Nel pomeriggio prosecuzione per Roma. □ *Cena ed alloggio in hotel.*

14° giorno (sabato) - ROMA • *Prima colazione* in hotel e termine dei nostri servizi.

C. Travel brochure: Italia con Polvani. ⭐ ⭐ ☆

You're going on a four month holiday to Europe. To start your holiday off, you've organised a bus tour of Italy. You'll fly directly to Rome where you'll be picked up by a Polvani bus. From the brochure try to work out answers to the following questions. On the map of Italy on page 17 label the cities you will be visiting and outline your journey.

ITALIA con POLVANI

1. Pick the dates for your tour.   Tour _____ Inizio _____ Termine _____

2. What season will it be?_____

3. Presuming you will be sharing a double room, how much will the tour cost in Italian currency?_____

   About how much would that be in Australian money?_____

4. Where will you spend your Fridays?_____

5. For how many days will you be in Rome?_____

6. Will you be going outside Italy? If so where?_____

7. Will you be visiting an island? If so, which one?_____

8. Which cities are called: la "città eterna" _____   la "città del giglio" _____

   Find out what these two expressions mean:_____

9. Which ancient Roman city will you be visiting? _____ What do you know about it?_____

   _____

10. Name some of the places of interest in Rome and Florence._____

    _____

    _____

11. Name some of the cities on the Italian Riviera (i.e. the north-western coast)._____

    _____

D. Quick Quiz. No looking in other books! How much do you know about Italy? ⭐ ⭐

1. What is the capital of Italy?

_____

2. Name Italy's unit of currency?

_____

3. Which two large islands are part of Italy?

_____

4. What are the names of the two volcanoes in Italy?

_____

5. What are the mountains in the north of Italy called?

_____

6. Which is the longest river in Italy?

_____

7. Name four Italian car manufacturers.

_____

_____

8. Name two Italian clothing manufacturers.

_____

9. What is bocce?

_____

10. Name a typical Italian dish (NOT pizza!).

_____

Suggested cultural background reading:
If you answered these questions correctly, you already know quite a few things about Italy. To find out more about Italy's history and culture, it is recommended that you work your way through **Regions of Italy** (CIS Educational). In each chapter of this workbook we will suggest that you read a section of **Regions of Italy** that will help build your background knowledge. To start with read "Introduction to Italy" pages 4-8 and do the puzzles and questions on pages 9 and 10.

E. Using the map of the twenty regions (Regions of Italy page 8) work out ⭐ ⭐
in which region you would find the cities that should be marked on the map on page 17.

🔲 Roma _____Lazio_____

1. Milano_____

2. Agrigento_____

3. Costa Smeralda_____

4. Firenze_____

5. Venezia_____

6. San Remo_____

7. Sulmona_____

8. Bologna_____

9. Siena_____

10. Modica_____

11. Pisa_____

12. Norcia_____

13. Lucca_____

14. Capri_____

CAPITOLO DUE

LA PARTENZA

ASCOLTIAMO

A. Listen to these people identifying the characters by what they are wearing. ★★ From the list below, circle what they have on.

☑ Tuta   Maglia   Cappello   Cappotto   (Cravatta)   Jeans   (Vestito)   Calzini

1. Cappotto   Camicia   Cappello   Giubbotto   Pantaloncini   Cravatta   Maglia

2. Giubbotto   Jeans   Camicia   Pullover   Pigiama   Golfino   Scarpa   Giacca

3. Pigiama   Gonna   Pullover   Cappotto   Jeans   Golfino   Impermeabile   Tuta

4. Calzini   Cappotto   Maglia   Tuta   Cravatta   Sciarpa   Pigiama   Vestito

5. Gonna   Impermeabile   Giacca   Giubbotto   Jeans   Cappello   Camicetta

6. Cappello   Cravatta   Calzini   Cappotto   Gonna   Pantaloncini   Vestito

7. Sciarpa   Scarpe   Tuta   Cappotto   Cappello   Vestito   Impermeabile   Maglia

8. Calzini   Maglia   Pigiama   Pantaloni   Cappello   Cappotto   Giacca   Golfino

B. Tick the expression you hear: ★

☑ Questa valigia è piccolissima.   ✓

   Questa valigia è piccola   ☐

1. Mamma, sei veramente antiquata.   ☐

   Mamma, sei veramente antipatica.   ☐

2. Dario, sei più alto.   ☐

   Dario, sei più alto?   ☐

3. Questa valigia è veramente pesante.   ☐

   Questa valigia è troppo pesante.   ☐

4. Presto ragazzi, l'aereo è in partenza.   ☐

   Presto ragazze, l'aereo è in partenza.   ☐

5. Ma chi sei tu?   ☐

   Ma chi è Lei?   ☐

6. Faye, dormi troppo.   ☐

   Faye dorme troppo.   ☐

7. Molto lieto, signorina.   ☐

   Molto lieta, signorina.   ☐

8. È vero che Lei gioca per la Juventus.   ☐

   È vero che lui gioca per la Juventus.   ☐

A. Domande sul fumetto.
Answer in Italian these questions based on the cartoon script: ★

☑ C'è la Signora Casati? _Sì, c'è._

1. C'è il marito? _____

2. C'è Bertoldo? _____

3. C'è la mamma di Bertoldo? _____

4. C'è Salvatore? _____

5. C'è Laura? _____

6. C'è la mamma di Faye? _____

☑ Chi è sempre in ritardo? _Dario è sempre in ritardo._

7. Chi parla con Faye? _____

8. Chi parla con Dino Zoff? _____

9. Chi dorme? _____

10. Chi legge il giornale? _____

11. Chi è sfacciata? _____

12. Chi si mette il cappotto? _____

☑ L'aereo è in partenza? _Sì, è in partenza._

13. Angela è nervosa? _____

14. Giorgio è nervoso? _____

15. Dario è in tempo? _____

16. Kevin parla con Dino Zoff? _____

17. Paolo Rossi gioca per la Juventus? _____

18. Dino Zoff gioca per la Juventus? _____

B. Write the correct form of the indefinite article in front of the following: ★

☑ _un_ fratello   4. _____ sorella   8. _____ edicola

1. _____ maglia   5. _____ mese   9. _____ canzone

2. _____ anno   6. _____ giocatore   10. _____ squadra

3. _____ scherzo   7. _____ scandalo   11. _____ lezione

C. Write the correct form of the definite article in front of the following: ★

☺ __il__ calcio   4. _____ scandalo   8. _____ aula

1. _____ anno   5. _____ mese   9. _____ gioventù

2. _____ fratello   6. _____ partita   10. _____ zaino

3. _____ sorella   7. _____ canzone   11. _____ classe

D. Write the correct form of questo in front of the following: ★

☺ __questa__ maglia   4. _____ mese   8. _____ canzone

1. _____ zaino   5. _____ squadra   9. _____ scherzo

2. _____ giocatore   6. _____ aula   10. _____ partita

3. _____ edicola   7. _____ anno   11. _____ astuccio

E. Adjectives (meanings, agreement). ★★
Apply the descriptions below to the person or thing depicted after each statement:

☺ Il marito è bruno.   _La signora Casati è bruna._

1. Il fratello è alto e giovane. _____

2. Laura è un po' sfacciata. _____

3. Questa tuta è molto elegante. _____

4. Lo zaino è così pesante, così pieno. _____

5. Cabrini è veramente simpatico. _____

6. Il cappotto è rosso. _____

F. Present tense of regular verbs.

Parl**are** to speak		Ved**ere** to see		Dorm**ire** to sleep	
parl**o**	I speak	ved**o**	I see	dorm**o**	I sleep
parl**i**	you speak	ved**i**	you see	dorm**i**	you sleep
parl**a**	he, she it speaks	ved**e**	he, she, it sees	dorm**e**	he, she, it sleeps
	you speak (formal)		you see (formal)		you sleep (formal)

WARNING:

Giocare keeps the same hard -**k**- sound throughout so it adds an -**h**- next to -**i** or -**e**.
e.g. gio**co**
   gio**chi**
   gio**ca**

But **leggere** doesn't take an -**h**-. It changes its sound next to -**i** or -**e**.
e.g. leg**go**
   leg**gi**
   leg**ge**

Complete this table: ★

	Parlare	Vedere	Dormire
io	parlo		
tu		vedi	
lui/lei			dorme

G. Complete the following sentences by writing the correct <u>present tense</u> form of the verb given in brackets: ★

☑ Kevin ___*parla*___ (parlare) con Dino Zoff.

1. Dino Zoff _____ (giocare) per la Juventus.

2. Kevin, è vero che tu _____ (segnare) 1.19 gol per partita?

3. Cabrini _____ (dormire) durante il volo.

4. Il signor Zoff _____ (leggere) in giornale.

5. Scusa, Dario, ma perchè _____ (leggere) questa rivista?

6. Sì, gioco al calcio ma non _____ (segnare) molti gol.

7. Se leggo un po' _____ (dormire) sempre bene.

8. Angela, tu _____ (parlare) italiano molto bene.

Leggi o giochi?

H. Irregular Verbs.

> **Andare is an *irregular verb.*** You'll have to learn it on its own.
> **Andare**   to go
> **vado**   I go
> **vai**   you go
> **va**   he, she, it goes
> **andiamo** we go
> **andate**   you (pl.) go
> **vanno**   they go

Complete the following table of <u>irregular verbs</u>: ★

	Essere	Avere	Andare
io	sono		
tu		hai	
lui/lei			va
noi		abbiamo	
voi	siete		
loro			

I. Complete the following sentences by writing the appropriate form of <u>andare</u>: ★

☑ Chi è quello? ___*Vado*___ a domandare.

1. Dunque, Dino, anche tu _____ in Italia?

2. Angela _____ a parlare con Dino Zoff.

3. Noi _____ a Roma e a Venezia.

4. Tardelli e Cabrini _____ in Italia con la squadra.

5. Voi _____ in Europa?

6. Ho bisogno di un giornale. _____ a vedere se c'è un'edicola.

J. Più.

> **Più** means <u>more</u>. Watch how it is used in the following sentences:
> **Il marito è ridicolo ma quest'uomo è più ridicolo.** The husband is ridiculous but this man is more ridiculous.
> **Il marito è alto ma quest'uomo è più alto.** The husband is tall but this man is taller.
>
> Italians can't add <u>-er</u> to an adjective. They always use **più**.
> **Non più** means <u>no longer, not...any more.</u>
> e.g. **Non gioco più.** I no longer play, I don't play any more.

Write down the Italian equivalent of the following: ★★
1. Dario is taller and thinner.

_____

2. Angela is not much (molto) taller.

_____

3. Who is more intelligent, Giorgio or Kevin?

_____

4. This man is younger and fairer.

_____

5. Mrs. Casati is darker and more elegant.

_____

6. Dino Zoff no longer plays for Juventus.

_____

7. They no longer go to Rome. _____

8. I don't go to school any more. _____

K. Clothes, colours. Give a description of the clothes worn by each of the following characters in Chapter 2 (pages 28-32 in the textbook). ★★★

☑ Cabrini _è con la giacca azzurra e i pantaloni grigi._

1. Bertoldo_____

2. La signora Casati_____

3. Laura_____

4. L'hostess_____

5. Dino Zoff_____

6. Kevin_____

7. Angela (at beginning)_____

8. Angela (at end)_____

L. Subject Pronouns.

io	I
tu	you
lui	he
lei	she
Lei	you (formal)

It is not necessary to use *subject pronouns* with Italian verbs,
since the ending of the verb generally makes clear who is doing the action.

e.g. **Gioco al calcio.** The **-o** ending signals that **I** am the one who is playing.
Giochi al calcio? The **-i** ending signals that I'm asking the question about **you.**
Gioca al calcio The **-a** ending signals that a **he** or **she** is playing.
(Whether it is he or she is usually clear from the context)

The pronouns are used when you need to emphasise the subject:

e.g. **Lui legge, lei dorme.** He's reading, she's sleeping.
Se tu non vai, io non vado. If you don't go, I'm not going.
Angela?!! Lei non è molto sfacciata. Angela?!! She's not very cheeky.

Subject pronouns are commonly used with **anche** meaning <u>too, also</u>.

e.g. **Anch'io vado a Roma.** I'm going to Rome too.
Parla italiano anche lei. She speaks Italian too.

You have to suppose that in the following cases the <u>subject</u> of the verb needs <u>special emphasis</u>. ★★
Supply the appropriate pronouns:

☑ Ah, ecco Dario! Forse *lui* ha una rivista.

1. Una rivista?!? Ma _____ non leggo durante il volo.

2. Scusi, signore, è vero che _____ gioca per l'Inter?

3. Conosci Kevin? Anche _____ va in Italia.

4. _____ non hanno molto tempo.

5. Anche _____ andiamo a Roma.

6. Avete una cintura di sicurezza anche _____?

7. _____ è molto alto, signore.

M. Parole Nuove. ★

1. Which of the colours won't you find on the Italian flag?

    bianco   rosso   azzurro   verde

2. If Cabrini plays for Juventus and Italy this year which colour won't he be wearing on the field?

    bianco   rosso   azzurro   nero

3. Which might be a bit too informal for a wedding?

    la giacca   la gonna   la tuta   la cravatta

4. Which number would come next?

    tre   sette   undici   quindici   _____

5. Which number is missing?

    due   tre   cinque   otto   _____   diciassette

6. Which can't score a goal?

    il giocatore   la squadra   la punta   la partita

N

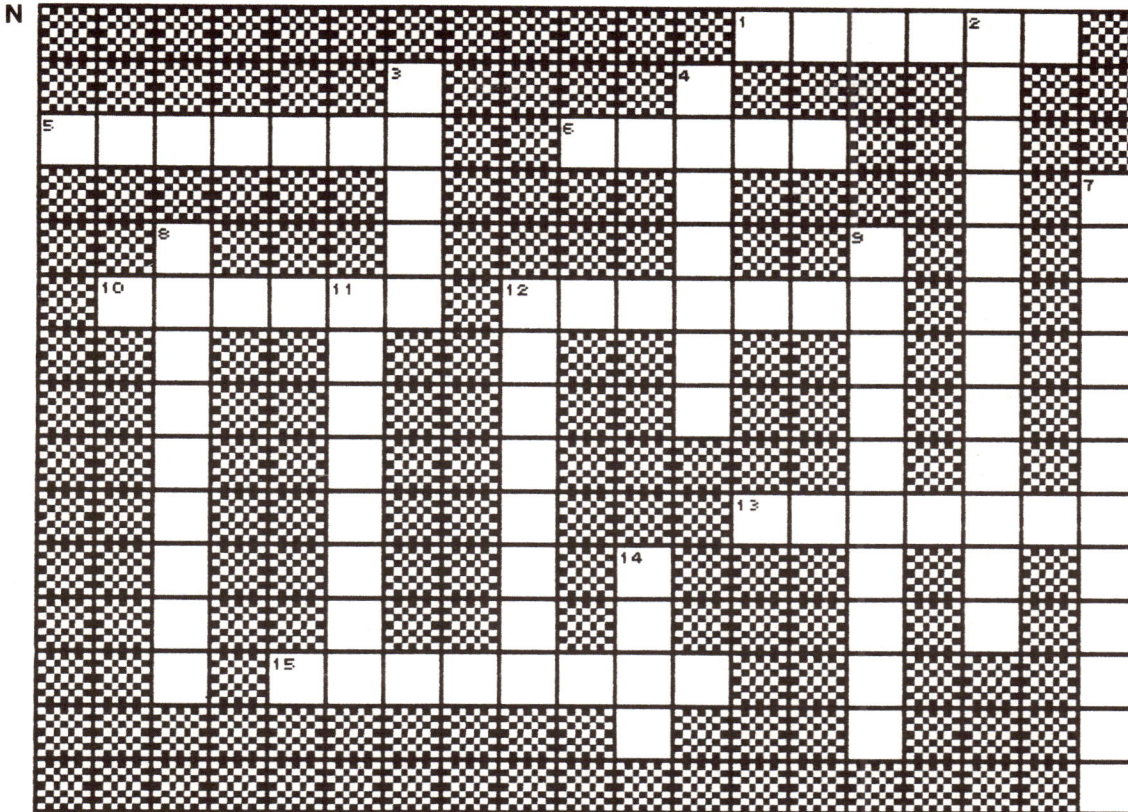

**Parole crociate –
abbigliamento.**

Orizzontali
1. Jumper
5. Dress/suit
6. Jeans
10. Jacket
12. Shirt
13. Cardigan
15. Coat

Verticali
2. Raincoat
3. Skirt
4. Socks
7. Shorts
8. Vest
9. Handkerchief
11. Tie
12. Hat
14. Tracksuit

O. How did Angela say? ★★

1. What don't you believe?_____

_____

2. Who is that with the blue jacket? He's really nice._____

_____

3. And the one who is reading the newspaper?_____

_____

4. Is it true that you play for Juventus?_____

P. How would you say? ★★★

1. What don't you see?_____

_____

2. Who is that with the yellow shirt? He's really tall._____

_____

3. And the one who is scoring the goal?_____

_____

4. Is it true you speak Italian?_____

Q. Ways of saying you.

| tu |
| Lei |

Italians have a *formal* and an *informal* way of addressing one another.
When talking to members of their family or to friends they use the **tu** forms.

e.g. **Mamma, sei veramente antipatica!**
Giorgio, non hai bisogno di tutto questo!

When talking to people they don't know very well they use the **Lei** form.

e.g. **Scusi, è vero che Lei gioca per la Juventus?**
Scusi, signora, Lei legge questo giornale?

☛ If you don't use the **Lei** forms with adults you don't know very well, what you're saying will sound too familiar, even a bit rude.

☛ It takes a while to get used to the **Lei** forms - at first it feels like you're talking about someone, not to someone.

☛ Notice that when using formal language, Italians often use the pronoun **Lei** in front of the verb - much more often than they use **tu.**

☛ When adults address young people they use the **tu** forms.
e.g. **Piacere, Kevin. Anche tu giochi al calcio?**
Young people always use the **tu** forms with one another.

☛ When you're addressing more than one person you use the **voi** forms.
Voi is used in both formal and informal situations.
e.g. **Presto, siete in ritardo! Avete solo venti minuti.**

You've just been introduced to Dino Zoff but you're having trouble getting used to the formal (Lei) form of address. You keep having to correct yourself. ★★

☑ Sei veramente alto.

Scusi, *Lei è veramente alto.*

1. È vero che giochi per la Juventus?

Scusi,_____

2. Dormi durante il volo?

Scusi,_____

3. Hai una valigia pesante?

Scusi,_____

4. Vai in Italia?

Scusi,_____

5. Parli inglese?

Scusi,_____

6. Leggi questa rivista?

Scusi,_____

7. Segni molti gol? **Scusi,**_____

8. Sei molto simpatico, Dino. **Scusi,**_____

R.

(crossword grid with partially filled letters: I, S, O, O, E, R, A)

★★

Parole crociate – numeri e colori.

Orizzontali
2. The colour of a famous panther
4. Sei più cinque
6. Unlucky in Australia, not in Italy
9. An easy Italian colour to remember
10. A pure colour
12. The number of regions in Italy
14. The colour of hope
15. Yellow

Verticali
1. The last of the teens
3. Similar to 9 orizzontale
5. A dozen
7. Makes a bull charge
8. Sixteen
11. Another shade of 3 verticale
13. Some italians wear this colour when they are mourning

S. Express the following in Italian: ★★★

1. Laura, you're really cheeky.

2. We are ready to take off.

3. Perhaps we have a scandal.

4. Where is Dario? Dario isn't here.

5. I'm not really nervous, I'm not afraid.

6. Are you going to Rome, Giorgio?

7. Well, are we all here?

8. Are you going to see Juventus, Kevin?

9. If we go to Italy, I'm going to Venice.

10. She has a new suitcase because she's going to Europe.

T. Imagine that you're joining Mrs. Casati and the gang for their four month stay in Italy. Make a list of:

a) Clothes you would take:	**b) Clothes you would have to buy:**
to take **da portare**	to buy **da comprare**

U. Here is a glimpse of Angela's wardrobe. Colour in her clothes according to the description provided: ★

Angela ha una gonna marrone, una sciarpa marrone e gialla,
calzini viola, scarpe verdi, un golfino arancione,
un fazzoletto rosa, pantaloncini arancione, impermeabile grigio,
tuta celeste e rossa, e cappello azzurro, rosso e viola.

V.

Parole crociate – riassunto. ⭐⭐⭐

Orizzontali
3. The person you know best
4. New
5. I'm going
6. Month
10. A close relative
12. Pleased to meet you (2 words)
13. I'm not afraid (3 words)
14. My
16. A score in football
17. Who?
20. Always
22. To go
23. You go (sing.)
24. Cheeky
25. Day

Verticali
1. That
2. What?
3. . . . vado
5. True
7. Quiet!
8. Who are they? (3 words)
9. I
10. Team
11. Year
12. My
15. Excuse me!
18. Greetings
19. Dark
21. Pleased to meet you
23. I see

W. Un po' di tutto. ★★★

If you can express the following in Italian you can feel confident that you have mastered the material in Chapter 2. The letter in brackets refers to a Parliamo exercise which you should find helpful.

1. Mrs. Casati is tall and Bertoldo is tall too. (A)

_____

2. It's not the brother, he's not so young. (B)

_____

3. The husband is strong but this man is stronger. (C)

_____

4. I don't believe it, that's Marco's sister. (D)

_____

5. My name is Irene and this is Marco. (E,F)

_____

6. I play for Juventus but he doesn't play. (G,H)

_____

7. Madam, do you speak Italian? (I)

_____

8. He needs a suitcase too. (J)

_____

9. I'm going to Rome and he is going too. (K,L)

_____

10. We're going to Italy. Are they going too? (K,L)

_____

X. Componimento. ★★★

Write a brief letter of introduction for a friend who will be staying with an aunt of yours in Italy. In your letter, mention:
▶ what he looks like and what he'll be wearing (so she'll recognise him when she picks him up)
▶ some of his good and bad qualities
▶ things he does.
HINT: **porterà** he'll be wearing

_____

_____

_____

_____

_____

_____

A. Parliamo con le mani. ★★

Pick an appropriate gesture from the Cultural Unit, **Parliamo con le mani** (pages 36-37 in the textbook) to respond to the following situations. Write the corresponding expression in the spaces below.
(Sometimes you will find more than one may be appropriate)

☺ Your friend is complaining that his sandwiches are dull, colourless and boring.

Che cosa ci possiamo fare!

1. You are trying to explain a plan for raising money to a not-too-bright friend.

2. Your friend finally understands and approves wholeheartedly!

3. Another friend thinks you've finally cracked up.

4. Now your friend is offering to sell you a second-hand tape.

5. Another of your many friends is raving on endlessly about something.

6. Someone is asking you what you think of his/her new bike.

Now practise them together with the appropriate gestures.

B. La Lavanderia.

You work in a dry cleaners in Sorrento. Someone brought in lots of clothes and now you have to fill out the receipt. Here is a list of items you cleaned: 2 skirts, 3 jumpers, 3 pairs of trousers, 1 jacket, a tracksuit, a raincoat, and 10 handkerchiefs.
In the left hand column write the number of items and in the right hand column write the amount in lire (you'll have to take a guess). Some items may not already be printed, you'll have to handwrite those in the empty lines.

DI MAIO GILDA "Lavanderia"
Sede: VIA P. R. GIULIANI n. 11
Dom. Fisc.: VIA S. NICOLA n. 12
80067 SORRENTO (NA)
C. F. DMO GLD 40C70 I862H
P. I.V.A. 04292360635

RICEVUTA FISCALE
(D.M. 28 Gennaio 1983)

n. _____

data 3/8

Nome
Signora Russo

QUANTITÀ, NATURA E QUALITÀ DEI SERVIZI

	CORRISPETTIVO IVA INCLUSA
Lavaggio (kg./capi)	
Giacche	
Pantaloni	
Gonne	
Paletots / Impermeabili	
Camicie	
Maglie / Golf	
Stiratura	
Capi in pelle	
Coperte / Tende	

Y 8385802 A/83

TOTALE L.

Corrispettivo non pagato L.

MOD. 6180.2(b) - Buffetti Grafica spa - via di Villa Bonelli, 21 - Roma - Aut. min. n. 384179/79 del 30.8.1979

ATTENZIONE:
il Piccolo Mercato
Via Armenia. 7 - angolo Via Traiano di fronte Alfa Romeo - Tel. 3870234 - MILANO

inizia
una

→

GRANDE
SVENDITA

con sconti dal 30 al 70%

DAL 29
GIUGNO

ABBIGLIAMENTO UOMO — DONNA E RAGAZZO
PANTALONI — JEANS — GONNE — CAMICETTE — MAGLIERIA
— GIUBBOTTI --
GRANDE ASSORTIMENTO DI SCAMPOLI

ALCUNI ESEMPI

PANTALONI			
JEANS	da L	9.900
GONNE	da L	9.900
MAGLIE	da L	9.900
CAMICETTE	da L	5.900
GIUBBOTTI	da L	9.900
COMPLETI	da L	19.000
	da L	9.900

E TANTI ALTRI ARTICOLI A PREZZI DI REALIZZO
GRANDE ASSORTIMENTO

TUTTO A PREZZI DI REALIZZO
APPROFITTATENE!
INGRESSO LIBERO

Organizzazione pubblicitaria GODINO EUGENIO - tel. (0321) 454666 - Novara

Avvisato Il Comune di Milano

C. Il Piccolo Mercato. ★★★

Extra vocabulary:

angolo	corner
di fronte	opposite
giubbotto	jacket – vest
ingresso	entrance
libero	free
mercato	market
sconti	discounts
svendita	sale

1. On what date did the sale start?_____

2. Exactly where is the market? (Including street and any helpful hints.)_____

_____

3. What do they sell opposite the market?_____

4. What items cost from 9.900 lire?_____

5. How much do jumpers cost?_____

6. How much does it cost to get in?_____

7. Find the Italian words for: large range_____

discounts from 30% to 70%_____

Suggested cultural background reading:
Regions of Italy, pages 17-19, Trentino – Alto Adige.

CAPITOLO TRE
IL TERRORISTA

ASCOLTIAMO

A. Listen carefully. What would you say to these people?

☑ Sei fifone	Sei ghiottone	Sei spiritoso	(Sei pazzo)	Sei un ficcanaso
1. Sei fifone	Sei ghiottone	Sei spiritoso	Sei pazzo	Sei un ficcanaso
2. Sei fifone	Sei ghiottone	Sei spiritoso	Sei pazzo	Sei un ficcanaso
3. Sei fifone	Sei ghiottone	Sei spiritoso	Sei pazzo	Sei un ficcanaso
4. Sei fifone	Sei ghiottone	Sei spiritoso	Sei pazzo	Sei un ficcanaso
5. Sei fifone	Sei ghiottone	Sei spiritoso	Sei pazzo	Sei un ficcanaso
6. Sei fifone	Sei ghiottone	Sei spiritoso	Sei pazzo	Sei un ficcanaso
7. Sei fifone	Sei ghiottone	Sei spiritoso	Sei pazzo	Sei un ficcanaso
8. Sei fifone	Sei ghiottone	Sei spiritoso	Sei pazzo	Sei un ficcanaso
9. Sei fifone	Sei ghiottone	Sei spiritoso	Sei pazzo	Sei un ficcanaso
10. Sei fifone	Sei ghiottone	Sei spiritoso	Sei pazzo	Sei un ficcanaso

B. What are they saying about the characters? Circle the word you hear being used to describe each person:

☑ **Faye:**	antiquata	(differente)	piccola	sciocca
1. **Angela:**	alta	simpatica	antipatica	elegante
2. **Kevin:**	intelligente	pigro	magro	piccolo
3. **Dario:**	simpatico	stupido	bravo	differente
4. **Laura:**	gentile	magra	birichina	spiritosa
5. **Giorgio:**	antipatico	antiquato	stanco	matto
6. **Signora Casati:**	vecchia	bionda	alta	antiquata

C. What are these people doing? Listen to what they say and circle the verb you hear them use:

☑ apro	(finisco)	ricevo	sento	chiamo
1. arrivo	pulisco	capisco	compro	prendo
2. aspetto	cerco	mangio	leggo	arresto
3. metto	gioco	piango	parto	preferisco
4. guardo	fumo	dormo	credo	arrossisco
5. trovo	arrivo	aspetto	capisco	sento
6. pulisco	piango	guardo	leggo	mangio

Suggested cultural background reading: Regions of Italy, pages 28-31, Marche.

SCRIVIAMO

A. Domande sul fumetto.

The following are important question words in Italian:

dove   where?
quando   when?
che cosa what?
chi   who?

Answer the following questions in Italian:

1. Dove sono i ragazzi?_____

2. Chi cerca un terrorista?_____

3. Dove bisogna mettere le valige?_____

4. Che cos'è piena e pesante?_____

5. Chi è molto gentile?_____

6. Che cosa mangia Mario?_____

7. Quando ha fame Mario?_____

8. Quando fuma Gaetano?_____

B. Plural of nouns.

	singular	plural
masculine	-o	-i
masc. + fem.	-e	-i
feminine	-a	-e

Nouns ending in **-o** in the singular usually form their plural in **-i**.
e.g. ragazz**o** → ragazz**i**
Most nouns that follow this pattern are *masculine*.

Nouns ending in **-a** in the singular usually form their plural in **-e**.
e.g. bomb**a** → bomb**e**
Most nouns that follow this pattern are *feminine*.

Nouns ending in **-e** in the singular usually form their plural in **-i**.
e.g. carabinier**e** → carabinier**i** (m)
    stazion**e** → stazion**i** (f)
Nouns that follow this pattern may be either *masculine* or *feminine*.

* There are some nouns denoting occupations which end in **-ista**.
If a male person is referred to, the noun is masculine and forms its plural in **-i**.
e.g. terrorist**a** → terrorist**i**
If a female person is referred to the noun is feminine and forms its plural in **-e**.
e.g. tennist**a** → tennist**e**

* Some nouns ending in **-cio, -gio, -cia, -gia** form their plurals in **-ci, -gi, -ce, -ge**.
e.g. vali**gia** → vali**ge**

Some nouns add an **-h-** to the plural.
e.g. banco → ban**chi**
    lago → la**ghi**

Write why you think this is so:_____

Write the following nouns in the plural:

☺ ragazzo _ragazzi_   4. scherzo_____   8. dentista_____   12. banco_____

1. aeroporto_____   5. storia_____   9. canzone_____   13. dente_____

2. studente_____   6. partita_____   10. aula_____   14. gamba_____

3. pallone_____   7. edicola_____   11. valigia_____   15. scandalo_____

C. Plural of definite article.

	singular	plural
masculine	il	i
	l'	gli
	lo	
feminine	la	le
	l'	

Masculine:

i   Before a *consonant* the masculine plural article is **i**.
e.g. **i** ragazzi

gli   Before a *vowel* the masculine plural article is **gli**.
e.g. **gli** italiani

gli   Also used before **s** + *consonant* or **z**.
e.g. **gli s**tudenti, **gli z**ii

Feminine:

le   The feminine plural article is always **le**.
e.g. **le** domande, **le** aule, **le** storie, **le** zie.

	masculine	feminine
At a glance	il ragazzo → i ragazzi il carabiniere → i carabinieri l'animale → gli animali lo zio → gli zii lo studente → gli studenti il terrorista → i terroristi	la domanda → le domande la canzone → le canzoni l'aula → le aule la zia → le zie la storia → le storie la tennista → le tenniste

Write the correct <u>definite article</u> in front of the following: ★

☺ _l'_ animale   3. _____ valige   6. _____ pallone   9. _____ scandali

1. _____ carabinieri   4. _____ australiani   7. _____ partita   10. _____ aule

2. _____ aeroporto   5. _____ australiane   8. _____ studentesse   11. _____ panini

D. Write the correct <u>definite article</u> in front of the following:

☺ _gli_ zii   3. _____ palloni   6. _____ edicola   9. _____ studenti

1. _____ storia   4. _____ canzoni   7. _____ tenniste   10. _____ studentesse

2. _____ scherzi   5. _____ animali (m)   8. _____ studente   11. _____ dente

E. Plural of nouns and articles. Write the following in the plural: ★

☺ il volo _i voli_   4. il giornalista_____   8. l'australiano_____

1. il ragazzo_____   5. la valigia_____   9. lo scherzo_____

2. l'aeroporto_____   6. la bomba_____   10. l'edicola_____

3. il carabiniere_____   7. il pallone_____   11. la valigia_____

F. Write the following in the plural: ⭐

◻ la ragazza *le ragazze*

1. l'australiana_____

2. la storia_____

3. il giornale_____

4. lo zaino_____

5. la giornalista_____

6. il doganiere_____

7. la canzone_____

8. l'aula_____

9. il banco_____

10. la sorella_____

11. la tennista_____

G. Plural of adjectives.

Some adjectives follow this pattern:

	singular	plural
masculine	-o	-i
feminine	-a	-e

e.g. il ragazz**o** alt**o**, la ragazz**a** alt**a**,
i ragazz**i** alt**i**, le ragazz**e** alt**e**.

Others follow this pattern:

	singular	plural
masculine	-e	-i
feminine		

e.g. il ragazz**o** intelligent**e**, la ragazz**a** intelligent**e**,
i ragazz**i** intelligent**i**, le ragazz**e** intelligent**i**.

Rewrite the following sentences in the plural: ⭐⭐

◻ Il doganiere è pazzo. *I doganieri sono pazzi.*

◻ La canzone è ridicola. *Le canzoni sono ridicole.*

◻ La valigia è pesante. *Le valige sono pesanti.*

1. Il carabiniere è alto._____

2. La canzone è vecchia._____

3. Lo zaino è pesante._____

4. La valigia è marrone._____

5. La gonna è ridicola._____

6. L'italiano è famoso._____

7. Il giornalista è russo._____

8. Il pallone è verde._____

9. La ragazza è australiana._____

H. Complete the following sentences by writing the correct verb form for the infinitive in brackets. ⭐⭐
Refer to L on page 41. Read the whole sentence before you decide what form to use!!!

◻ Il carabiniere ____*mette*____ (mettere) la bomba sopra il banco.

1. Giorgio e Angela _____ (parlare) italiano.

2. Se siamo stanchi _____ (dormire) durante il volo.

3. _____ (dormire) bene quando sono stanco.

4. _____ (mettere) la bomba sopra il banco????? Sei scemo!!!

5. Il cane _____ (dormire) all'aeroporto.

l'aeroporto

6. _____ (parlare) solo inglese??? Siete pigri!!!

7. Ragazzi, presto, _____ (mettere) il pallone in questa valigia!!!

8. Chi _____ (parlare) italiano in classe?

9. Il robot _____ (ricevere) la palla.

10. I tennisti _____ (mangiare) i pani.

I. Parole crociate - le nazioni e le lingue.

Orizzontali
2. She speaks
7. Rome is it's capital
9. Girl who lives in Perth.
12. It's capital is Beijing
14. Someone who lives in Paris.
16. Australians speak this language.
17. A man from Frankfurt.
18. Someone from Amsterdam.
20. . . . spagnolo
21. . . . arabi
22. It's capital is Washington.

Verticali
1. I ragazzi . . . (parlare) italiano
3. . . . Giappone.
4. . . . Grecia.
5. Someone from Athens.
6. The language of Hong Kong.
8. A woman from Bari.
10. Spoken by people in Barcellona.
11. Nation to the east of Italy.
13. Michelangelo spoke this language.
15. People in Moscow speak this language.
19. O, something is missing in the Netherlands!

J. Molto meaning <u>very</u>.

When **molto** means <u>very</u>, it's an *adverb*, so it never changes its ending. All *adverbs* in Italian are *invariable*.
e.g. Siamo **molto** stanchi.
     Le ragazze sono **molto** belle.

Remember: If **molto** means <u>a lot</u>, it's an *adjective*, so it has to agree with the noun.
e.g. Ci sono molt**e** ragazz**e**.

Rewrite the following sentences in the plural: ★ ★

☺ Il ragazzo è molto stanco. *I ragazzi sono molto stanchi.*

1. L'australiano è molto forte.

2. Questa ragazza è intelligente.

3. La valigia è molto pesante.

4. La maglia è gialla e verde.

5. Il giornalista non è inglese.

6. L'aula è molto grande.

7. La ragazza è molto magra.

8. Lo studente è molto nervoso.

K. Lei form (revision). ★ ★

Faye is very slow to catch on to the Italian way of using the formal **Lei** verb forms with people other than family or close friends. She keeps using the familiar **tu** forms, even with adults she has just met. You'll have to correct her:

☺ Faye: Sei molto gentile. *Lei è molto gentile.*

1. Faye: Sei un terrorista o un giornalista?

2. Faye: Hai paura quando trovi una bomba?

3. Faye: Quando arrivi in Italia?

4. Faye: È vero che aspetti una famosa tennista?

5. Faye: Dormi bene quando sei molto stanco?

6. Faye: Perchè non mangi? Non hai fame?

7. Faye: Se perdi questo terrorista sei fritto!

8. Faye: Perchè non prendi una limonata se hai sete?

L. Present tense of regular verbs.

Parlare to speak	Mettere to put	Dormire to sleep
parlo	metto	dormo
parli	metti	dormi
parla	mette	dorme
parliamo	mettiamo	dormiamo
parlate	mettete	dormite
parlano	mettono	dormono
e.g. fumare, giocare arrivare, aspettare	e.g perdere, credere prendere, vedere	e.g. sentire, aprire

Choose a verb from the lists above to express the following: ★

☺ I speak   *parlo*

1. they sleep_____

2. you (sing.) speak_____

3. I am speaking_____

4. they are putting_____

5. it's sleeping_____

6. we put_____

7. he sleeps_____

8. you (pl.) put_____

9. she sleeps_____

10. we're speaking_____

11. you (pl.) speak_____

Why are verbs ending in **-care, -gare, -cere, -gere a little different?**_____
_____

In what way are the following verbs different?

mangiare:_____

cercare:_____

piangere:_____

M. Present tense + revision. Express the following in Italian: ★★★

1. I'm Australian but I speak Italian.
_____

2. Where are you putting the suitcases, Gino?
_____

3. Excuse me, Sir. Do you hear a bomb? _____

4. We don't play soccer any more. _____

5. Mario, Gaetano, do you see the terrorist?
_____

6. The carabinieri open Kevin's suitcase.
_____

7. They lose twenty minutes at Rome airport.
_____

8. She arrives dead tired with a heavy suitcase.
_____

N. Complete the following sentences by writing the correct verb form for the infinitive in brackets: ★★

1. I ragazzi _____ (arrivare) stanchi morti all'aeroporto.

2. Il giornalista _____ (aspettare) una tennista famosa.

3. Scusi, signore, non sono sicuro. Dove _____ (mettere) la valigia?

4. Presto, ragazzi, _____ (aprire) tutte le valige!

5. Ma signore, i ragazzi _____ (essere) stanchi e _____ (avere) fame.

6. _____ (cercare) una bomba qui??!! Siete pazzi!!!

7. Ma dai, Mario, _____ (mangiare) sempre. _____ (essere) un vero ghiottone.

8. I giornalisti _____ (perdere) tempo perchè _____ (parlare) con Laura.

9. Giorgio, Dario, zitti!!! _____ (piangere) sempre.

10. Non siamo bambini, non _____ (piangere).

O. Avere *expressions*.

> **Quanti anni hai?** How old are you?
> When an Italian asks how old someone is he is really asking how many years the person has.
> In reply, the person will say that he or she has a certain number of years.
> e.g. **Mario, quanti anni hai?** Mario, how old are you?
> **Ho quarantatrè anni.** I'm forty-three (years old).
> **E Lei, signora, quanti anni ha?** And how old are you, madam?
> **Quanti anni hanno Giorgio e Laura?** How old are Giorgio and Laura?

Write the Italian for the following: ★★

1. Excuse me, sir, how old are you?_____

2. I'm twenty-eight, nearly twenty-nine._____

3. Giancarlo is seventeen._____

4. Giulia isn't twenty-one._____

5. You're the captain and you're only nineteen!!??_____

_____

6. If you're fifteen, I'm eighteen._____

_____

7. How old are Renato and Daniela?_____

8. Dino Zoff is forty or forty-one years old._____

_____

9. Are you sure you're only fifteen?_____

_____

10. How old are you (pl.)?_____

P. More expressions with avere.

avere caldo	to be hot	**avere paura**	to be afraid
avere fame	to be hungry	**avere ragione**	to be right
avere freddo	to be cold	**avere sete**	to be thirsty
avere fretta	to be in a hurry	**avere torto**	to be wrong

e.g. **Sono stanco e ho fame.**   I'm tired and hungry.
    Il capitano ha ragione; sei pazzo.   The captain is right; you're crazy.
    Chi ha paura di questa bomba?   Who's afraid of this bomb?

* Remember also: **avere bisogno di** to need
e.g. **Ho bisogno di aiuto.** I need help.

Express the following in Italian: ★★★

1. She is eighteen.

2. They are wrong.

3. I'm cold.

4. Are you afraid, Sir?

5. You're right, Mario.

6. Are you in a hurry, boys?

7. He's not hungry.

8. We're hot.

9. They need help.

Q. Avere Expressions. Express the following in Italian: ★★★

1. But sir, we're all so tired and we're in a hurry.

2. Giulia is only three but she's not scared.

3. Yes, I'm hungry, but pasta is a bit heavy.

4. Boys, if you're cold I have two jumpers here.

5. You're right! This newspaper is old.

6. We're not afraid, we're strong.

7. The journalists are in a hurry.

8. Are you thirsty, girls?

9. The policeman is wrong. Kevin isn't a terrorist.

R. Express the following in Italian: ★★★

1. How are you?_____

2. How old are you?_____

3. I'm well, thanks._____

4. I'm fourteen._____

5. I'm tired._____

6. I'm thirsty._____

7. I have a heavy suitcase._____

8. I have twenty minutes._____

S. Distinguishing <u>verbal</u> from <u>adjectival</u> expressions.

Study the following examples:

I am tired	**sono stanco**	I am sleeping	**dormo**
he's crazy	**è pazzo**	he's eating	**mangia**
we are old	**siamo vecchi**	we are leaving	**partiamo**
they're kind	**sono gentili**	they're reading	**leggono**

How would you explain the difference between the sentences on the left and those on the right?

_____

_____

What do you have to be very careful about when you are expressing the continuous present (am sleeping, is reading, are leaving, etc.) in Italian?

_____

Write the Italian for the following: ★★★

1. Renato is very tired; he's sleeping at the airport.

_____

2. Roberta is hungry but she's not eating.

_____

3. Yes, we're Australian but we're speaking Italian.

_____

4. Juventus is not playing here, the players are leaving for Sydney.

_____

5. She is very intelligent; she is speaking Italian very well.

_____

6. She is playing basketball because she is tall.

_____

T. Revision. Express the following in Italian: ★★★

1. Renato's backpack is extremely full. He's going to Rome.

_____

2. Gaetano is smoking. He always smokes when he's scared.

_____

3. They're going to school but they're late. They have ten minutes.

_____

4. Are you sure she has everything? She's waiting at the airport.

_____

5. You're crazy. You don't need six jumpers. I'm hot!

_____

6. You're right. This overcoat is really heavy.

_____

U. Parole crociate – revision.

Orizzontali

2. Pleased to meet you! Molto . . .
5. Certainly not!
8. . . . . italiani
10. Another word for nazione.
11. Also
13. That's enough!
15. Ugly
16. . . . . doganiere
18. Six
20. I'm going
21. Open up!
23. I have
26. Magazine
28. Quite well!
30. I am
32. Near
33. Only

Verticali

1. She goes
2. Light
3. You
4. Who is it? (2 words)
6. How boring! (2 words)
7. . . . .palla.
9. A, an
11. You're a real pain!
12. You (sing.) have
14. Now
17. Polite form
19. . . . . studente
22. Hurry!
23. They have
24. Plural of la
25. With
27. Everything
29. They are
31. We

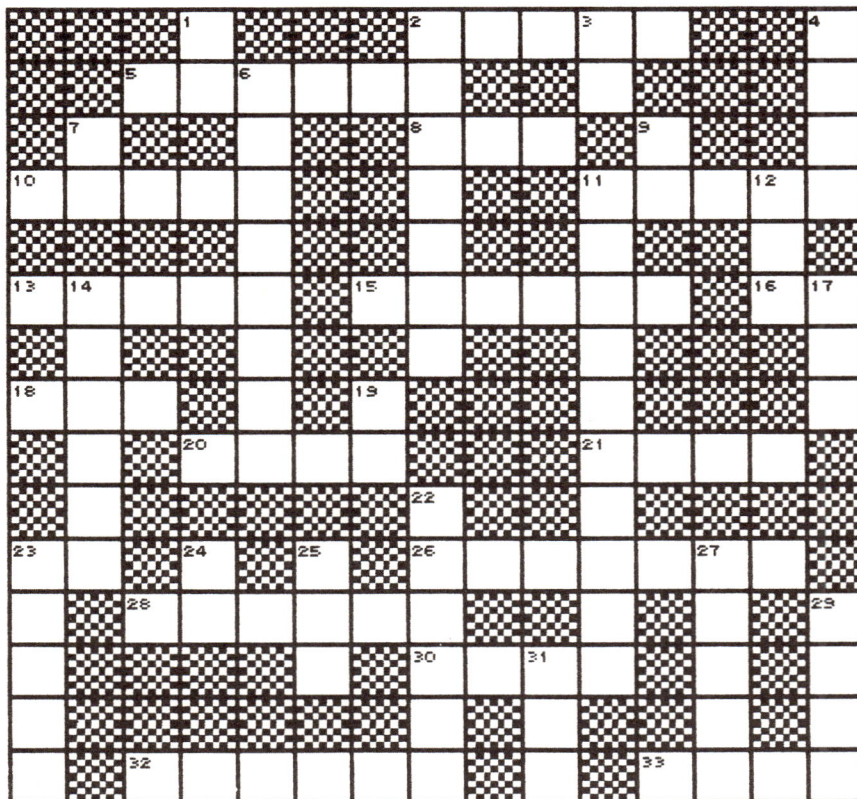

SCRIVIAMO

V. Words ending in -ista.

Like the -ist ending in English (tourist, motorist, dentist, etc.) the **-ista** ending is often used with Italian nouns which denote a person engaged in some occupation or activity.
e.g. il terror**ista**, la tenn**ista**
   i terror**isti**, le tenn**iste**
Remember that these words are masculine when they refer to a male person, feminine when they refer to a female.
Work out the English meaning for each of the words below and then write the plural in Italian: ★

☑ la giornalista *the journalist* *le giornaliste*

☑ il barista *the barman* *i baristi*

1. l'artista (f) _____ _____

2. l'autista (m) _____ _____

3. il chitarrista _____ _____

4. il ciclista _____ _____

5. la linguista _____ _____

6. il fascista _____ _____

7. il turista _____ _____

8. il romanista _____ _____

W. See if you can work out the Italian equivalents of the following: ★★

1. telephonist_____
2. pharmacist_____
3. nudist_____
4. pessimist_____
5. capitalist_____
6. feminist_____
7. pianist_____
8. dentist_____
9. violinist_____
10. specialist_____
11. florist_____
12. optimist_____

X. How did they say . . . If you can't remember how the cartoon characters expressed the following in Italian, why not check the cartoon story? ★★

1. Is it necessary to open all the suitcases?_____

2. Quick, kids, open the suitcases!_____

3. But sir, we're all so tired, we're hungry, we're thirsty._____

4. I'm sorry, sir. You are very kind._____

5. If you lose this terrorist you've had it._____

6. Just a moment. Can't you see I'm eating?_____

7. It's not true. I only eat when I'm hungry._____

8. You play with this? You're crazy!_____

Y. How would you say . . . ★★★

1. Is it necessary to look for the terrorist?

_____

2. Quick, kids, put the cases on the bench.

_____

3. But sir, they're all hot, thirsty, and tired.

_____

4. I'm sorry, sir. You are very nice (likeable).

_____

5. If we lose this bomb we've had it!

_____

6. Just a moment, Mario. Can't you see I'm reading this paper?

_____

7. It's not true. I only sleep when I'm tired.

_____

8. She plays with this? She's crazy!

_____

Z. Write a sentence stating the nationality of the people below and the language they speak:

1. _Questa è una ragazza australiana che parla inglese._

2. _____

3. _____

4. _____

5. _____

6. _____

AA. Un po' di tutto.

If you can express the following in English you can feel confident that you have mastered the material in Chapter 3. The letter in brackets refers to a Parliamo exercise which you should find helpful.

1. I'm sorry, but it's necessary to catch the plane immediately. (A)_____

_____

2. It's not true, I don't sleep all the time. (B)_____

3. We always lose everything. We're crazy! (C)_____

4. All the children are playing tennis. (D)_____

5. They read the papers but they don't believe all the stories. (E)_____

_____

6. Excuse me, sir, are you Italian? (F)_____

7. Excuse me, madam, are you leaving today or tomorrow? (G)_____

_____

8. She's tired and hungry. (H)_____

9. Where are the magazines and newspapers? (I)_____

10. All the backpacks are heavy. (J)_____

BB. Componimento.

Remember that friend of yours who is going to stay with your aunt in Italy? (See page 32 if you don't.) Well, your mother has asked you to write down some information about each member of your family for aunty – after all, it's over six years since she came to Australia for a visit. For each person write down: age, description, what he or she does.

☑ Sandro: *ha sedici anni, è alto e biondo. Gioca a tennis.*

_____

_____

_____

_____

_____

_____

_____

_____

_____

_____

_____

_____

A. Zoff: 40 anni e non sentirli.

1. What is Dino Zoff advertising?

_____

2. Why did they choose him to do the advertisement?

_____

3. What does he claim that Cuore does for him?

_____

4. Cuore has vitamins and is poly-unsaturated. According to the advertisement, why is this important?

_____

_____

Dino Zoff: 40 anni e non sentirli.

Dino Zoff, campione del mondo:
"Olio Cuore da molti anni mi aiuta a stare in forma." Cuore è un olio di semi di mais dietetico, saporito, leggero, gustoso. Arricchito con vitamina E e vitamina B6, olio Cuore ha un'alta percentuale di componenti grassi insaturi. E questo è importante per la tua efficienza di oggi e di domani.

Mangiar bene per sentirsi in forma.

Olio Cuore, solo dal cuore del mais.

B. Your uncle who has just retired has decided to go on a trip to Italy. He has written to the travel agency and received the schedule on page 51. Since he doesn't understand Italian he's asked you to interpret for him. ★★★

1. Where do I have to go to pick up the start of the tour?_____

_____

2. I'll be arriving in Italy on July 3rd. On what day and what date will the next tour leave?_____

_____

3. I'll be travelling alone and I don't want to share a room. How much will the tour cost me?_____

   Could you give me a rough idea in dollars?_____

4. I don't want to be rushed. Will I have much time in each city?_____

_____

_____

5. On which day will we see the Leaning Tower?_____

6. How much time will I spend in Rome, and what will I see?_____

_____

_____

7. Will I see any of the South of Italy?_____

_____

8. Will we see any of that lovely countryside in central Italy?_____

_____

9. The 14th of July is my birthday, what will I be doing on that day?_____

_____

_____

10. Teach me a couple of Italian phrases that might come in handy._____

_____

_____

_____

_____

Gemme d'Italia partenze da Milano

Tour TOPAZIO (ogni lunedì)				
Aprile	9	16	23	30
Maggio	7	14	21	28
Giugno	4	11	18	25
Luglio	2	9	16	23	30
Agosto	6	13	20	27
Settembre	3	10	17	24
Ottobre	1	8	15	22

Tour Topazio

Milano - Genova - Pisa - Siena - Roma - Napoli - Sorrento - Capri - Roma - Assisi - Firenze - Ravenna - Padova - Venezia - Verona - Milano

Partenze: ogni lunedì

1° giorno - Ritrovo dei partecipanti a **Milano**, alle ore 8.30 presso l'hotel Hilton, Via Galvani 12. Partenza per **Genova**, visita della città, seconda colazione e proseguimento lungo la Riviera di Levante fino a **Pisa**. Cena e pernottamento in albergo.

2° giorno - Prima colazione in albergo. Subito dopo visita alla Piazza dei Miracoli per ammirare la Cattedrale, il Battistero, la Torre Pendente. Partenza per **Siena**. Seconda colazione in ristorante e visita alla Piazza del Campo, la Cattedrale, il Municipio, ecc. Nel pomeriggio proseguimento per **Roma**. Cena e pernottamento

3° giorno - Prima colazione e pernottamento in albergo. Al mattino visita alla città (Quirinale, Fontana di Trevi, Pantheon, Castel Sant'Angelo, Vaticano, S. Pietro). Al pomeriggio escursione facoltativa a Tivoli.

4° e 5° giorno - Prima colazione e pernottamento in albergo. Giornate a disposizione per visite e escursioni facoltative.

6° giorno - Dopo la prima colazione partenza per **Napoli**. Breve giro città e visita a Pompei. Seconda colazione in ristorante. Proseguimento per **Sorrento**. Sistemazione in albergo, cena e pernottamento.

7° giorno - Subito dopo la prima colazione partenza con battello per **Capri**. Tempo permettendo visita alla Grotta Azzurra. Salita alla Piazzetta di Capri e seconda colazione in ristorante. Nel pomeriggio ritorno a Sorrento, indi a **Roma** con cena lungo la strada. Pernottamento in albergo.

8° giorno - Dopo la prima colazione partenza per **Assisi**. All'arrivo visita della città comprendente la Basilica di S. Francesco, la Chiesa di S. Chiara e altri monumenti religiosi. Seconda colazione in ristorante. Indi proseguimento per Perugia, il lago Trasimeno e la campagna toscana fino a **Firenze**. Cena e pernottamento in albergo. Escursione facoltativa a San Gimignano.

9° giorno - Prima colazione, cena e pernottamento in albergo. Al mattino visita della città comprendente Piazza della Signoria, Palazzo Vecchio, gli Uffizi, la Cattedrale, il Battistero, il Ponte Vecchio, l'Accademia delle Belle Arti. Pomeriggio a disposizione.

10° giorno - Dopo la prima colazione partenza verso il Nord e l'Adriatico fino a **Ravenna**. Visita e seconda colazione. Indi proseguimento per **Padova**, in tempo per visitare la Basilica di S. Antonio. Partenza per **Venezia**. Trasferimento da Piazzale Roma con vaporetto all'albergo. Resto del pomeriggio a disposizione. Cena e pernottamento in albergo.

11° giorno - Prima colazione, cena e pernottamento in albergo. In mattinata visita della città a piedi comprendente la Basilica di S. Marco, il Campanile, il Palazzo Ducale, il Ponte dei Sospiri. Pomeriggio a disposizione. Escursione facoltativa alle isole della laguna.

12° giorno - Prima colazione e trasferimento con vaporetto a Piazzale Roma. Proseguimento in autopullman per **Verona** dove si visiterà la pittoresca Piazza delle Erbe, il centro storico, l'arena, ecc. Seconda colazione e partenza per **Milano** dove termina il viaggio.

Quota individuale di partecipaz. L. 1.134.000

Supplemento camera singola L. 194.000

ASCOLTIAMO

A. Listen for the weather forecast being given for different cities of the world and circle the appropriate word/s:

🔊 **Bali:**	vento	~~afa~~ (circled)	pioggia	caldo	neve
1. **Madrid:**	caldo	neve	nevica	nuvoloso	piove
2. **Tokio:**	aria inquinata	piove	aria pura	afa	caldo
3. **Londra:**	pioggia	nevica	vento	caldo	nuvoloso
4. **Bombay:**	freddo	caldo	afa	pioggia	temporale
5. **Toronto:**	nevica	aria pura	vento	afa	freddo
6. **Francoforte:**	freddo	temporale	piove	nuvoloso	caldo
7. **Hong Kong:**	freddo	fresco	vento	caldo	aria pura
8. **Cortina D'Ampezzo:**	aria pura	aria fresca	freddo	aria inquinata	vento
9. **Roma:**	caldo	freddo	afa	piove	nuvoloso
10. **Lima:**	nevica	temporale	nuvoloso	freddo	vento

B. Tick the expression you hear.

🔊 Ci sono molti giornalisti qui oggi. ✓

    C'è un giornalista qui oggi. ☐

1. Dario preferisce dormire. ☐
    Dario, preferisci dormire? ☐

2. Piangi sempre quando perdi? ☐
    Piangi sempre quando perde? ☐

3. È un ragazzo intelligentissimo. ☐
    Quel ragazzo è intelligentissimo. ☐

4. C'è un carabiniere qui? ☐
    C'è un cameriere qui? ☐

5. Quanti tennisti ci sono in questo posto? ☐
    Quante tenniste ci sono in questo posto? ☐

6. Questo zaino è vecchissimo. ☐
    Questo zaino è pienissimo. ☐

7. Finisce sempre alle sei. ☐
    Finisci sempre alle sei. ☐

8. Laura è veramente sfacciata. ☐
    Laura è veramente sfacciata? ☐

A. Domande sul fumetto. Answer the following questions in Italian:

1. Dov'è Laura?_____

2. Quando mangia molto Laura?_____

3. Laura parla solo inglese?_____

4. Ci sono molti campi da tennis in Australia?_____

5. Che cosa gioca Laura?_____

6. I giornalisti chi cercano?_____

7. Perchè la signora Casati ha fretta?_____

B. Comprehension of cartoon script. From the alternatives given below, choose and rewrite the sentence which best retells what has happened in the last two chapters. Rewrite the sentences you choose without starting a new line for each and without numbering them. ⭐⭐

1. a) I ragazzi sono stanchissimi quando arrivano all'aeroporto di Roma.
   b) Dopo un volo di ventitrè ore tutti i ragazzi sono morti.
2. a) Trovano molti giornalisti e una tennista australiana.
   b) Trovano che i carabinieri cercano un terrorista.
3. a) Bisogna aprire tutte le valige.
   b) Il doganiere apre la valigia di Kevin.
4. a) Prende il pallone per una bomba.
   b) Trova una bomba e chiama i carabinieri.
5. a) I carabinieri prendono Angela per il terrorista.
   b) I carabinieri arrestano gli studenti australiani.
6. a) Il giornalista scrive che i carabinieri sono scemi.
   b) Un giornalista guarda e scrive questa storia per un giornale.
7. a) I giornalisti prendono Laura per una famosa tennista.
   b) I giornalisti prendono Laura per una ragazza irlandese.
8. a) Lei trova che bisogna rispondere a molte domande.
   b) Laura piange quando ha una dieta speciale.
9. a) Laura e i ragazzi prendono l'autobus per Roma.
   b) La signora Casati piange perchè non dorme bene.

_____

_____

_____

_____

_____

_____

_____

_____

_____

If you have written down the correct alternative in each case, you should now have your own summary of the cartoon script for Chapters 3 and 4.

C. C'è, ci sono.

C'è means <u>there is</u>. In a question it means <u>is there?</u>
The plural of c'è is ci sono.
e.g. Scusi, <u>c'è</u> un volo per Roma oggi?
   Excuse me, <u>is there</u> a flight to Rome today?
   No, mi dispiace, ma <u>ci sono</u> due voli domani.
   No, I'm sorry, but <u>there are</u> two flights tomorrow.

Answer the following questions in Italian, saying that "<u>There are many...</u>": ★★

☺ C'è un volo per Londra oggi? _Sì, ci sono molti voli per Londra oggi._

1. C'è un gabinetto all'aeroporto?

_____

2. C'è un campo da tennis a Roma?

_____

3. C'è una partita durante l'inverno?

_____

4. C'è un giocatore tedesco in questa squadra?

_____

5. C'è un'intervista con i giocatori in questo giornale?

_____

D. More on the Lei form of address. ★★

Look at the interview between the journalists and Laura the tennis star. They don't know her as Laura, as Mrs. Casati and the others do; they have to call her **signorina**. They can't use the *familiar* ways of saying <u>you are, you have, you speak, you play</u>, etc. They have to use the *formal* ways of saying *you*.
If Dario were questioning Laura he would put the questions in the following ways.
Next to his questions you write the way the journalists asked them.

☺ Faye, sei irlandese o australiana?   _Signorina, Lei è irlandese o australiana?_

1. Parli italiano? _____

2. Hai una dieta o mangi un po' di tutto? _____

3. Giochi sempre a tennis? _____

4. Preferisci il doppio o il singolo? _____

5. Piangi quando perdi? _____

6. Pulisci le scarpe o metti scarpe nuove? _____

7. Trovi che l'Italia è bella? _____

8. Vai a Roma oggi? _____

9. Sei stanca e hai fame? _____

10. Ami lo sport? _____

E. Laura was so overwhelmed by the reporters' questions that she left many of them unanswered. Write down the answers that you think she would have given to these questions: ★★

1. Ci sono molti campi da tennis in Australia?

_____

2. Riceve molte lettere dai tifosi italiani?

_____

3. Dorme bene quando c'è un torneo importante?

_____

4. Preferisce il singolo o il doppio?

_____

5. Piange quando perde?

_____

6. Trova che l'Italia è bella?

_____

Now see if you can make up three questions of your own. ★★★

1._____

2._____

3._____

F. Asking questions.

You're already familiar with the most common way of asking questions. You use exactly the same word order as a statement but write a question mark at the end of the sentence. If you're speaking you just make it sound like a question.
e.g. Questo è un pallone.
Questo è un pallone?
* Another way of forming a question is by inverting the sentence so that it starts with the verb.
e.g. **È un pallone questo?**
Remember:
In English you use the word <u>do</u> when forming a question.
In Italian <u>do</u> is never translated.
Do you sleep well? **Dormi bene?**

Rewrite these questions in the inverted form:

☑ Il giornalista è contento?___È contento il giornalista?_____

1. I carabinieri cercano un terrorista?_____

2. Laura è sfacciata?_____

3. Il giornalista è all'aeroporto?_____

4. La signora Casati cerca Laura?_____

G. See if you can work out which questions were asked to receive the answers below. Use the **Lei** form of address. ★★

☒ *Lei mangia molto quando ha fame?* No, non mangio molto quando ho fame.

1. _____ No, non gioco sempre a tennis.

2. _____ Preferisco le scarpe vecchie.

3. _____ Sì, sono la tennista australiana O'Rally.

4. _____ L'autobus parte adesso.

5. _____ Gioco a tennis qui a Roma.

6. _____ I carabinieri arrivano subito.

Lei è un ghiottone!
Lei è pazzo!
Lei è ridicolo!

Ma, diamoci del **tu**!

H. Diamoci del tu.

You might sometimes find when you're speaking to an Italian that you are invited to drop the more formal **Lei** forms and to use the more familiar **tu** forms. He might say, **"Diamoci del tu"**, which means "Let's start using the **tu** forms with each other." The change from **Lei** to **tu** forms doesn't always happen in such an official way. More often than not, one person starts using the **tu** forms, the other person notices and replies in the same manner.

You find that you are being more formal than you need to be. The person you are speaking to wants to be on more familiar terms, so you repeat what you said, this time in the <u>tu</u> way. ★★

☒ Ha fame adesso?
   Ma, diamoci del tu! *Hai fame adesso?*

1. Ha una valigia molto pesante?
   Ma, diamoci del tu! _____

2. Non è molto in ritardo.
   Ma, diamoci del tu! _____

3. Lei parla italiano e francese?
   Ma, diamoci del tu! _____

4. Legge tutte queste riviste?
   Ma, diamoci del tu! _____

5. Ma Lei parte per Roma o per Milano?
   Ma, diamoci del tu! _____

6. Preferisce il rosso o il bianco?
   Ma, diamoci del tu! _____

7. Lei ha diciannove anni??!!
   Ma, diamoci del tu! _____

8. Lei è pazzo.
   Ma, diamoci del tu! _____

I. Express these questions in Italian:

1. Do they play tennis?_____

2. Does he think we're crazy?_____

3. Are you (pl.) cold?_____

4. Are you (sing.) going to the football match?_____

J. More about -ire verbs.

Dormire to sleep	Finire to finish
dormo	finisco
dormi	finisci
dorme	finisce
dormiamo	finiamo
dormite	finite
dormono	finiscono

Dormi bene quando viaggi in aereo?

So, there is a large group of **-ire** verbs which are ★
a bit different from the **dormire** type.
Which three letters are inserted between the stem
(or base part) of the verb and the ending?

_____

Which two parts of these verbs don't have these letters?

_____

When an **-o** follows the **-isc-** the sound is a hard **-isk-**.
How does the pronunciation change when the **-isc-** is
followed by an **i** or an **e?**

_____

Which common verbs have we seen of the **dormire** type?

_____

_____

_____

Which common verbs have we seen of the **finire** type?

_____

_____

_____

Write the Italian for the following: ★

1. he hears_____

2. they finish_____

3. I prefer_____

4. we sleep_____

5. she cleans_____

6. they open_____

7. I leave_____

8. we understand_____

9. you (sing.) open_____

10. you (pl.) prefer_____

11. I understand_____

12. they clean_____

K.

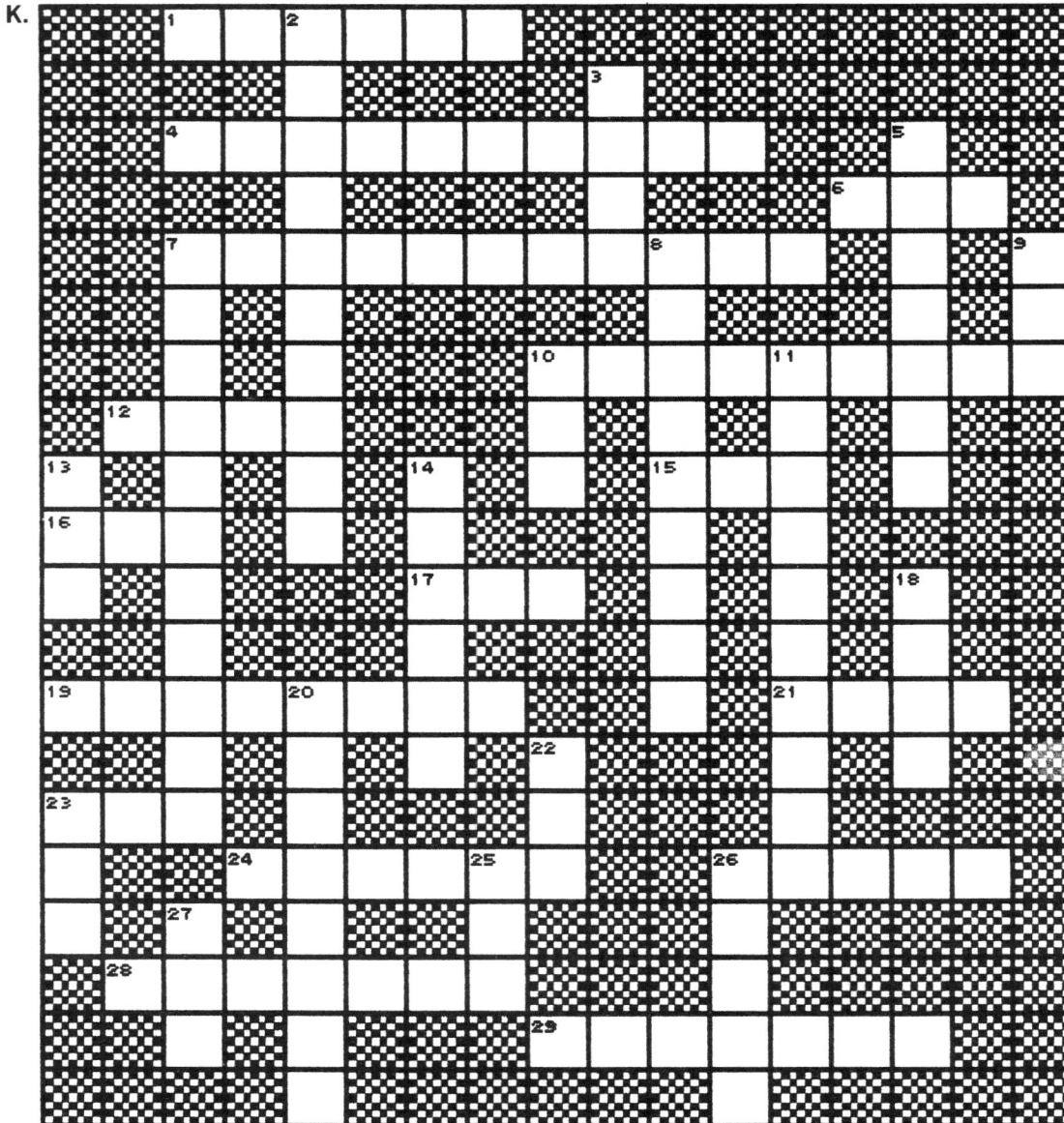

Parole crociate –
numeri 1 - 50. ★

Orizzontali
1. 11
4. 19
6. 2
7. 48
10. 38
12. 8
15. 3
16. 1
17. 2
19. 15
21. 9
23. 6
24. 5
26. 7
28. 21
29. 4

Verticali
2. 19
3. 9th
5. 4
7. 14
8. 33
9. 1
10. 3
11. 39
13. 2
14. 16
16. 1
18. 9
20. 18
22. 3
23. 6
25. 1
26. 7
27. 6

L. Present tense (revision).
Complete the following sentences by writing the correct verb form for the infinitive given in brackets. ★

1. I ragazzi _____ (mettere) le valige sopra il banco.

2. Scusa, Gina, _____ (preferire) il pallacanestro o il tennis?

3. A scuola noi _____ (avere) l'opportunità di praticare molti sport

4. Uei, ragazzi, dove _____ (andare) adesso?

5. Non siete stanchi perchè _____ (dormire) così bene.

6. Laura non _____ (capire) tutte quelle domande.

7. Ma ragazze, perchè non _____ (pulire) quelle scarpe?

8. Scusi, Capitano, ma Lei _____ (credere) questa storia ridicola?

SCRIVIAMO

M. Complete the following sentences by writing the correct verb form for the infinitive in brackets. ★

☺ Il carabiniere non ___*capisce*___ (capire) molto.

1. Mario _____ (finire) il panino e _____ (dormire) sopra il banco.

2. Se non _____ (capire) queste domande non sei intelligente.

3. Quando Laura gioca a tennis _____ (preferire) il singolo.

4. Sì, io _____ (capire) l'italiano ma non _____ (sentire) bene.

5. _____ (partire) adesso ma siamo in ritardo.

6. I carabinieri non _____ (sentire) la bomba.

N. Plurals of nouns, verbs, adjectives (revision). Change the following sentences from singular to plural: ★★

☺ Il carabiniere mangia quando ha fame.

I carabinieri mangiano quando hanno fame.

1. Il giornalista cerca la ragazza australiana.

_____

2. Il carabiniere apre la valigia nera.

_____

3. Uei ragazzo, tu sei pazzo.

_____

4. Questo zaino rosso è veramente pesante.

_____

5. La domanda è molto ridicola.

_____

6. Dove vai?

_____

7. Che cosa preferisci?

_____

8. Non va a Roma perchè ha paura.

_____

9. Accidenti! La domanda è troppo difficile.

_____

10. Perdo troppo tempo qui.

_____

O. Che.

> When you're asking a question the Italian word for <u>who</u> is **chi**.
>
> e.g. **Chi cerca un terrorista?**
>
> Another Italian word for <u>who</u> is **che**.
>
> You don't use it when you're asking a question but when you want to say something about someone you have already mentioned in your sentence.
>
> e.g. **I carabinieri cercano un terrorista <u>che</u> ha una bomba.**
>
> In the sentence above which word does **che** relate to?
>
> _____

Use the word **<u>che</u>** and then some extra information to complete the sentences below: ★★

☑ I carabinieri cercano un terrorista *che ha una bomba.* _____

1. Ci sono molti giornalisti_____

2. I ragazzi parlano con un doganiere_____

3. Mario è un carabiniere_____

4. Il giornalista scrive la storia di due carabinieri_____

5. Laura è una ragazza australiana_____

6. La signorina Karnitemova è una tennista russa_____

> **Che** can also mean <u>that</u>.
>
> e.g. **Il capitano crede <u>che</u> siamo scemi.** The captain thinks <u>that</u> we're silly.
>
> **Laura trova <u>che</u> l'Italia è bellissima.** Laura finds <u>that</u> Italy is very beautiful.

P. Parole nuove. ★

1. Which of these sports doesn't use a net?

   il calcio   il pallacanestro   il pallavolo   il nuoto

2. Which of these sports would be the most difficult to practise without a partner?

   il pattinaggio   la scherma   il nuoto   il ciclismo

3. Which number is missing?

   sei   tredici   ventuno   _____   quaranta

4. Which number is missing?

   cinquanta   quarantasette   quarantuno   ventinove   _____

5. Which number is missing?

   cinquanta   _____   trentadue   ventitrè   quattordici

6. Which expression would you not expect someone to use during a summer thunderstorm?

   c'è afa   c'è temporale   piove   nevica

7. During which season will Mrs. Casati and the gang spend most of their stay in Italy?

   l'autunno   l'inverno   la primavera   l'estate

8. Which expression best explains what a tifoso is?

   pratica molti sport   gioca al calcio   ama lo sport   una tennista russa

Q. Parole crociate – espressioni. ★★

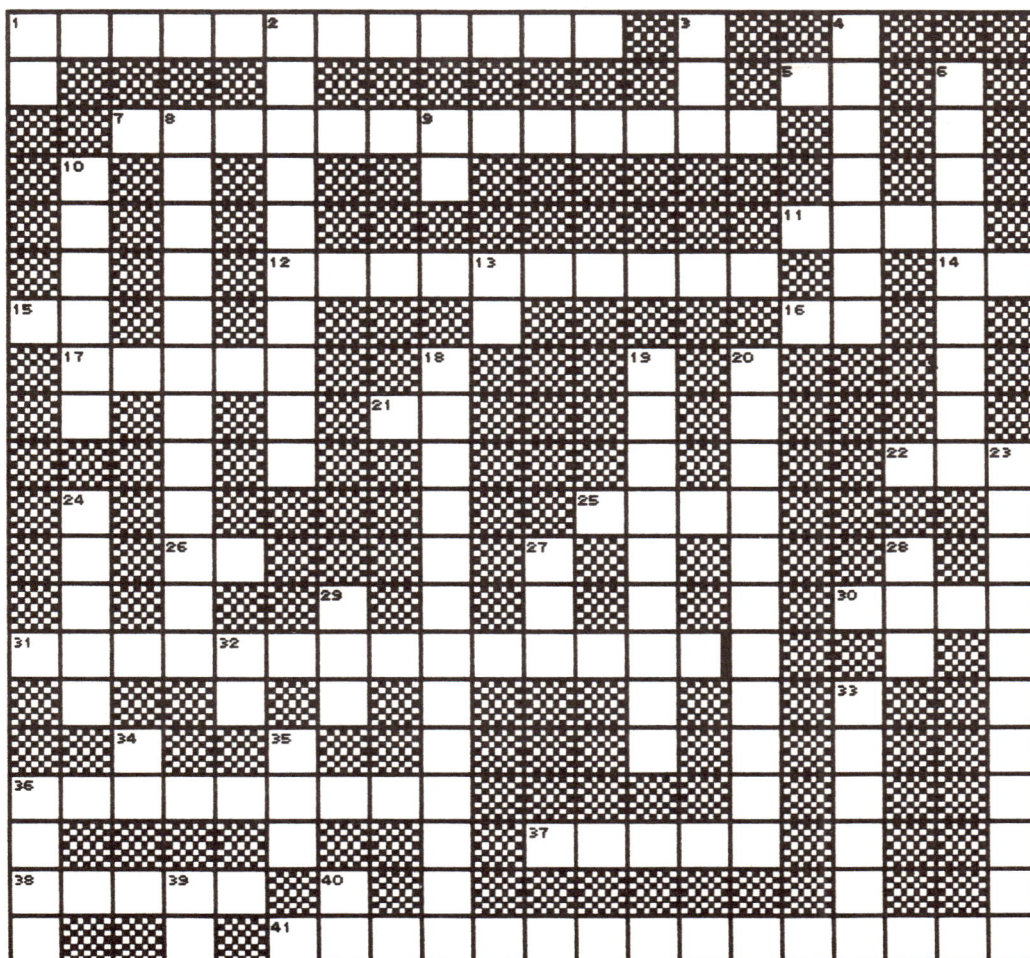

Orizzontali
1. Let's be less formal (3 words)
5. There are: ... sono
7. To jog (3 words)
11. Today
12. I'm sorry
14. Of
15. Feminine singular definite article
16. But
17. Swimming
21. Feminine plural definite article
22. More
25. They
26. Masculine singular definite article
30. After
31. I'm going to the country (3 words)
36. Not too bad (4 words)
37. Hot
38. Wind
41. You'd say this after running a marathon (3 words)

Verticali
1. From
2. What's the weather like? (3 words)
3. With
4. Rain
6. Good grief!
8. I'll be there shortly! (2 words)
9. It's hot: ... caldo
10. A procrastinator's favorite word
13. If
18. We're wasting our time! (2 words)
19. Hang on a moment! (2 words)
20. I need it! (3 words)
23. A little of everything (4 words)
24. Come off it! (2 words)
27. Sultriness
28. We
29. Skiing
32. Not out
33. Non fa caldo, fa ...
34. Vado ... città.
35. I love
36. Snow
39. You
40. Masculine definite article

R. Caldo, freddo (Aldo Paoletti). Read page 59 of your textbook.
Then when you've understood how to use è/fa freddo/caldo, write the Italian for the following: ★ ★

1. It's cold today. _____

2. I'm cold. _____

3. The water is very cold. _____

4. The coffee is hot. _____

5. I'm hot. _____

6. It's very hot today. _____

7. There is a thick fog today. _____

8. There are black clouds today. _____

S. Che tempo fa? Match the following expressions with the illustrations below: ★

C'è afa.   Fa molto freddo.   Nevica.   Piove.   C'è temporale.
C'è vento.   È nuvoloso.   L'aria è inquinata.   Il sole splende.

1. _____   2. _____   3. _____

4. _____   5. _____   6. _____

7. _____   8. _____   9. _____

SCRIVIAMO

T. Previsioni del tempo.
Examine the weather information closely, then answer the following questions in full:

PREVISIONI DEL TEMPO
a cura del servizio meteorologico dell'Aeronautica

TEMPERATURE IN ITALIA

ALGHERO	+12	+15
ANCONA	+ 4	+ 8
BARI	+10	+11
BOLOGNA	+ 2	+ 4
BOLZANO	− 7	+ 5
CAGLIARI	+15	+18
CAMPOBASSO	+ 3	+ 4
CATANIA	+13	+21
CUNEO	− 3	+ 2
FIRENZE	+ 3	+ 8
GENOVA	+ 1	+ 7
L'AQUILA	0	+ 6
MESSINA	+17	+19
MILANO LINATE	− 3	+ 7
NAPOLI	+10	+15
PALERMO	+21	+22
PERUGIA	+ 1	+ 4
PESCARA	+ 6	+ 8
PISA	+ 3	+11
POTENZA	+ 6	+12
REGGIO CALABRIA	+16	+19
ROMA FIUMICINO	+ 9	+10
ROMA URBE	+ 8	+10
S. MARIA DI LEUCA	+12	+17
TORINO	− 4	+ 6
TRIESTE	+ 4	+ 5
VENEZIA	− 1	+ 7
VERONA	− 1	+ 8

TEMPO PREVISTO per OGGI

MOLTO NUVOLOSO

AERONAUTICA MILITARE SERVIZIO METEOROLOGICO

FENOMENI
≡ nebbia ▽ rovesci
▨ piogge ⌐ temporali
✳ nevicate ▼ grandine

MARE
quasi calmo
poco mosso
mosso
molto mosso
agitato
molto agitato

VENTO
MODERATO → 10-20 nodi = forza 4-5
FORTE → 21-33 nodi = forza 6-7
MOLTO FORTE → 34-47 nodi = forza 8-9

E ALL'ESTERO

AMSTERDAM: sereno	− 2	+ 5
ATENE: nuvoloso	+11	+19
BANGKOK: sereno	+24	+32
BELGRADO: pioggia	+ 2	+ 6
BERLINO: nuvoloso	− 2	0
BRUXELLES: nuvoloso	0	+ 4
BUENOS AIRES: pioggia	+20	+28
CARACAS:	n.p.	n.p.
CHICAGO: nuvoloso	+ 7	+13
COPENAGHEN: nuvoloso	+ 1	+ 4
DUBLINO:	n.p.	n.p.
FRANCOFORTE: sereno	− 2	+ 1
GERUSALEMME: pioggia	+12	+24
GINEVRA: nuvoloso	− 1	+ 4
HELSINKI: sereno	− 1	+ 1
HONG KONG: sereno	+20	+23
IL CAIRO: nuvoloso	+15	+26
LIMA: sereno	+15	+21
LISBONA: sereno	+ 7	+16
LONDRA: nuvoloso	+ 5	+ 6
LOS ANGELES: nuvoloso	+10	+20
MADRID: sereno	+ 6	+14
MONTREAL: nuvoloso	− 1	+ 1
MOSCA: sereno	− 8	− 4
NUOVA DELHI: sereno	+11	+27
NEW YORK: sereno	+ 9	+17
OSLO: sereno	− 2	− 1
PARIGI: nuvoloso	+ 1	+ 9
PECHINO:	n.p.	n.p.
RIO DE JANEIRO: sereno	+15	+19
SAN FRANCISCO: nuvoloso	+ 9	+14
STOCCOLMA:	n.p.	n.p.
SYDNEY: sereno	+18	+29
TOKIO:	n.p.	n.p.
VARSAVIA: nuvoloso	− 3	+ 1
VIENNA: sereno	− 4	+ 5

EVOLUZIONE GENERALE: sul Mediterraneo permane una circolazione depressionaria. - **TEMPO PREVISTO:** Su tutte le regioni da molto nuvoloso a coperto con piogge estese, localmente anche di forte intensità, ed occasionali temporali più frequenti sulle regioni centro-meridionali. Nevicate sui rilievi del centro-nord, localmente anche a quota bassa. - **TEMPERATURA:** stazionaria su valori inferiori alla media stagionale. - **VENTI:** tra est e sud-est da moderati a forti. - **MARI:** da molto mossi ad agitati.

☑ Che tempo fa ad Atene?

Ad Atene è nuvoloso

1. È l'estate in Italia?

2. Che tempo fa in Italia oggi?

3. Dove in Italia fa più caldo?

4. Dove fa più freddo all'estero?

5. Come sono i mari?

6. C'è vento in Italia?

7. Piove in Sardegna?

8. Piove a Venezia?

9. Che tempo fa a Belgrado?

10. Che tempo fa a Sydney?

11. Dove fa più caldo all'estero?

U. Nationality.

In Italian, adjectives of nationality always begin with *small letters*.
e.g. **Dario è australiano.** Dario is Australian.

Nouns of nationality can begin with *small or capital letters*.
Note the use of the definite article **gli, i,** before the nouns.
e.g. **Gli italiani amano lo sport.** The Italians like sport.
I Francesi parlano francese. French people speak French.

N.B. The names of countries always begin with *capital letters*.
e.g. **Vado in Inghilterra.** I'm going to England.

The drawings below suggest sentences about sports played by people in different countries.
Write a sentence for each one. Remember that you use <u>giocare</u> a for some sports and <u>praticare</u> for others.

☺ Gli svedesi giocano a tennis.

1._____

2._____

3._____

4._____

5._____

6._____

V. Complete the following using the correct adjective of nationality (revision). ★

☺ Hans è di Amsterdam?   Sì, Hans è olandese.

1. Karl è di Amburgo?   _____

2. Charles è di Parigi?   _____

3. Charles è di Londra?   _____

4. Carlos è di Barcellona?   _____

5. Chuck è di Nuova York?   _____

6. Carlo è di Poggibonsi?   _____

7. Carl è di Vladivostok?   _____

8. Charlie è di Rockhampton?   _____

W. How did Laura say... ★★

1. When I'm hungry I eat a lot._____

2. No, I don't always play tennis._____

3. My name is Laura. Are you free this evening? Where are you going?_____

_____

4. Mrs. Casati, do you cry when you clean your shoes?_____

_____

X. How would you say... ★★★

1. When I'm not hungry I don't eat much.

_____

2. No, I don't always play basketball.

_____

3. What is your name? I'm free this evening. I'm going to Rome.

_____

4. I don't cry much and I don't clean my shoes.

_____

Y. La Ballata di Gino Zappalà.
Write vero or falso after the following statements relating to La Ballata di Gino Zappalà (page 60 textbook). ★★

1. Gino è alto e biondo. _____   6. Antonello è alto ma Gino è più alto. _____

2. Gino non è veramente modesto. _____   7. Gino è veramente ricco. _____

3. Faye non capisce che Gino è molto romantico. _____   8. Faye ama le Alfa Romeo. _____

4. Faye viaggia sempre in motorino. _____   9. Faye ama Gino. _____

5. Antonello vede Gino in città. _____   10. Faye va in città con Gino. _____

Z. Un po' di tutto.
If you can express the following in Italian you can feel confident that you have mastered the material in Chapter 4. In brackets you will find the letter of a Parliamo exercise which you should find helpful. ★★★

1. Gilda, why don't you clean these shoes? (A)

_____

2. They prefer the blue track suit. (B)

_____

3. He doesn't understand why we're opening the suitcases. (C)

_____

4. Rino? He's going to Italy too. (D)

_____

5. Excuse me, miss, do you play tennis? (E)

_____

6. These are the boys who are crying. (F)

_____

7. Is there a newspaper here? There are many newpapers here! (G)

_____

CONTINUA

8. All these stories are ridiculous. (H)

_____

9. Enrico eats a lot; he's always hungry. (I)

_____

10. It's muggy today: it's very warm and there's rain. (J)

_____

AA. Componimento.   ★★★

1. **Your parents have taken you to Italy in the middle of July. Write a short postcard to a classmate.**
   - Greet your friend (Caro/a ...) and ask how he/she is.
   - Explain where you are.
   - Say what the weather is like there and inquire about the weather back home.
   - Say what you're doing, what you're seeing, where you're going tomorrow.
     (It's perfectly alright to use the present tense when you're talking about domani).
   - Send your best wishes to another friend.

_____

_____

_____

_____

_____

_____

_____

2. **You're planning a letter to a new penfriend in Italy. You make a list of things you want to tell him/her about yourself and of questions you want to ask about him/her. Write your lists below:**

Questions about myself	Questions for him/her
_____	_____
_____	_____
_____	_____
_____	_____
_____	_____
_____	_____

If you can't think what to write consider age, what you look like, personality, sports you play, languages you speak, teams you barrack for, how much you eat. Use the vocabulary of this and previous chapters to help you.

A. Gli italiani amano lo sport. Vero o Falso (based on pages 56-57 of the textbook):

1. In Italia c'è molto sport alla televisione. _____

2. Quando c'è una partita internazionale di calcio alla televisione le strade sembrano vuote. _____

3. Tutti gli italiani preferiscono guardare piuttosto che praticare lo sport. _____

4. C'è una squadra di calcio che si chiama il Genova. _____

5. La Juventus ha vinto il campionato italiano molte volte. _____

6. Giocano a calcio al Foro Italico. _____

7. Il windsurf è uno sport popolare. _____

8. Il Giro d'Italia è una gara automobilistica. _____

9. Tutti gli studenti italiani devono praticare lo sport. _____

10. A Laura non piace giocare a pallacanestro. _____

B. Complete the following sentences by choosing an appropriate word or phrase from this list. ★★
The sentences are based on the Cultural Unit, Gli italiani amano lo sport, pages 56-57 of the textbook.

scudetti	alla televisione	il calcio	l'allenamento	l'ippica	praticare
una volta	allenarsi	Giro d'Italia	il ciclismo	allo stadio	tifosi

1. Lo sport preferito degli italiani è senza dubbio _____

2. Tutti guardano la partita _____, o se possono, vanno _____

3. La Juventus ha più _____ di tutte la altre squadre, forse perchè ha vinto il

   record numero di _____

4. L'Italia ha avuto grandi campioni di tennis ed ha anche vinto la Coppa Davis _____

5. _____, lo sport della bicicletta è un altro sport di grande importanza.

6. Le due gare più importanti per il ciclismo sono il "Tour de France" e il "_____"

7. Le scuole offrono l'opportunità di _____ molti sport.

8. Per essere in forma bisogna _____

9. Mi piace giocare a pallacanestro ma non mi piace _____

10. Altri sport popolari sono l'automobilismo e _____

C. Viaggi e sport. Vero o falso.   ★★

1. Il Gran Premio di Spagna è in autunno. _____

2. Il Gran Premio comincia venerdì il 27 aprile. _____

3. I ragazzi di dieci anni pagano di meno. _____

4. A Wimbledon non giocano di domenica. _____

5. Si gioca dalle 14.00 alle otto di sera. _____

6. La Nazionale italiana gioca contro la Turchia, a Roma. _____

7. La partita non vale per la coppa del mondo. _____

Suggested cultural background reading: Regions of Italy, pages 32-35, Puglia.

VIAGGI e SPORT

AMICHEVOLE TURCHIA - ITALIA

Viaggio a Istanbul dal 2 al 5 Marzo

2 Marzo/Venerdì: Nella tarda mattinata volo Milano o Roma - Istanbul. Arrivo in serata. Trasferimento in albergo. Inizio del soggiorno, basato sul trattamento di pernottamento e prima colazione.

3 Marzo/Sabato: Nel pomeriggio trasferimento allo stadio per assistere all'incontro di calcio Turchia-Italia.

4 Marzo/Domenica: In mattinata, visita della città.

5 Marzo/Lunedì: In mattinata, volo Istanbul - Milano o Roma.

Quota di partecipazione (minimo 20 partecipanti):
da Milano Lit. 550.000 / da Roma Lit. 510.000.
Riduzione ragazzi, inferiori ai 12 anni, Lit. 160.000.
Supplemento camera singola: Lit. 90.000.

IL TORNEO DI WIMBLEDON

Viaggio a Londra dal 28 Giugno al 1° Luglio

28 Giugno/Giovedì: In mattinata, volo Milano o Roma - Londra. All'arrivo, trasferimento in albergo. Inizio del soggiorno, basato sul trattamento di pernottamento e prima colazione continentale. **Pomeriggio a disposizione per recarsi a Wimbledon per assistere al più famoso torneo del mondo** (si gioca tutti i giorni, tranne la Domenica dalle 14.00 alle 20.00).

29-30 Giugno/Venerdì e Sabato: Giornate dedicate al Torneo di Wimbledon (Trasferimento libero, si consigliano taxi o metropolitana, stazione Southfields).

1° Luglio/Domenica: In mattinata, volo Londra - Milano o Roma.

Quota di partecipazione (minimo 20 partecipanti):
da Milano Lit. 660.000 / da Roma Lit. 750.000.
Riduzione ragazzi, inferiori ai 12 anni, Lit. 170.000.
Supplemento camera singola: Lit. 140.000.

GRAN PREMIO F.1. - SPAGNA

Viaggio a Malaga dal 27 al 30 Aprile

27 Aprile/Venerdì: In mattinata volo Milano o Roma - Malaga.
All'arrivo, trasferimento in albergo. Sistemazione nelle camere riservate. Inizio del soggiorno a Fuengirola, basato sul trattamento di pernottamento e prima colazione.

28-29 Aprile/Sabato e Domenica: Giornate a disposizione.

Per assistere alle prove ed al Gran Premio F.1.

30 Aprile/Lunedì: In mattinata, trasferimento in aeroporto e partenza per Milano o Roma.

Quota di partecipazione (minimo 20 partecipanti):
da Milano Lit. 670.000 / da Roma Lit. 690.000.
Riduzione ragazzi, inferiori ai 12 anni, Lit. 220.000.
Supplemento camera singola: Lit. 100.000.

IN COLLABORAZIONE CON *Alitalia* **E ALTRI VETTORI IATA**

PROMEMORIA:		CERIMONIA DI APERTURA	ATLETICA LEGGERA	CALCIO	CANOA	CANOTTAGGIO	CICLISMO	EQUITAZIONE	GINNASTICA	HOCKEY	JUDO	LOTTA	NUOTO	NUOTO SINCRONIZZATO	PALLACANESTRO	PALLAMANO	PALLANUOTO	PALLAVOLO	PENTATHLON MODERNO	PUGILATO	SCHERMA	SOLLEVAMENTO PESI	TIRO CON L'ARCO	TIRO A SEGNO	TIRO A VOLO	TUFFI	VELA	CERIMONIA DI CHIUSURA
28 SABATO	LUGLIO	•																										
29 DOMENICA	LUGLIO			•			•	•	•	•			•		•		•	•	•		•			•	•			
30 LUNEDÌ	LUGLIO			•		•	•	•	•		•	•			•		•	•			•			•	•			
31 MARTEDÌ	LUGLIO			•		•	•		•	•	•	•			•	•		•			•			•	•		•	
1 MERCOLEDÌ	AGOSTO			•		•	•	•	•			•			•	•	•		•	•		•		•	•		•	
2 GIOVEDÌ	AGOSTO			•		•	•	•	•			•			•	•	•	•	•	•	•			•	•			
3 VENERDÌ	AGOSTO		•	•		•	•		•	•		•			•	•		•			•			•	•		•	
4 SABATO	AGOSTO		•			•			•	•	•		•		•	•		•			•	•	•	•	•			
5 DOMENICA	AGOSTO		•	•			•		•	•	•	•			•	•		•			•	•				•		
6 LUNEDÌ	AGOSTO		•					•	•	•		•	•	•	•	•		•			•					•	•	
7 MARTEDÌ	AGOSTO		•				•		•	•	•		•	•		•	•			•	•	•				•	•	
8 MERCOLEDÌ	AGOSTO		•		•		•		•	•	•		•	•		•					•	•	•			•	•	
9 GIOVEDÌ	AGOSTO		•	•	•		•	•	•	•	•			•			•			•	•		•			•		
10 VENERDÌ	AGOSTO		•		•		•	•	•	•	•	•			•	•	•	•			•			•		•		
11 SABATO	AGOSTO		•	•	•			•	•	•						•					•					•		
12 DOMENICA	AGOSTO						•																			•		•

D. This is the timetable for the next Olympics. Answer the following questions about it in Italian: ★★★

☺ Quando comincia il ciclismo?

Comincia domenica il 29 luglio.

1. Quando comincia il canottaggio?

_____

2. Quando comincia il nuoto sincronizzato?

_____

3. Quando è la cerimonia di chiusura?

_____

4. Quanti giorni dura il pallacanestro?

_____

5. Quanti giorni dura il calcio?

_____

6. Quali sport praticano nell'acqua?

_____

7. Quale sport preferisci?

_____

8. Quali sport hanno bisogno di una palla?

_____

cominciare to begin   **durare** to last   **quale/i** which

CAPITOLO CINQUE

I MOTORINI

ASCOLTIAMO

A. There are plenty of things wrong with this car. Listen carefully for each item:

☑ camion	candele	(clacson)	freni	frizione
1. le luci	la ruota	l'acceleratore	l'aria	l'autista
2. l'olio	lo specchietto	l'aria	le candele	l'olio
3. la frizione	la targa	il motore	i fari	i freni
4. il clacson	la gomma	l'aria	i fari	l'acceleratore
5. le luci	il motorino	il motore	la multa	il sedile
6. il portabagagli	la ruota	il sedile	lo specchietto	la frizione
7. l'olio	le luci	la ruota	le candele	la batteria
8. la targa	la motocicletta	il motore	il volante	i fari
9. il garage	il guasto	l'acceleratore	l'aria	il sedile
10. i freni	la frizione	i fari	l'olio	la benzina

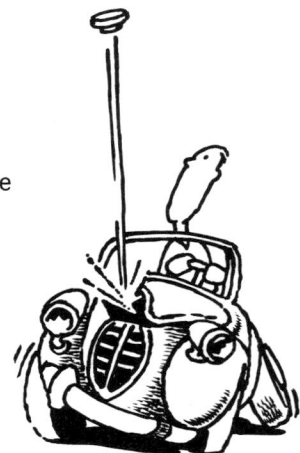

B. What's the date? Write in the spaces provided the dates you hear being said:

☑ *lunedì tre aprile*

1. _____
2. _____
3. _____
4. _____
5. _____
6. _____
7. _____
8. _____
9. _____
10. _____

SCRIVIAMO

A. Domande sul fumetto.

> **Question words:**
> **chi?** who? **che cosa?** what? **dove?** where?
> **perchè?** why? **quanti?** how many? **quando?** when?

The following questions refer to the comic strip. Answer them in Italian:

1. Chi visita un cugino a Roma?

2. Dove camminano i ragazzi?

3. Perchè è stanco Giorgio?

4. Perchè non sono stanchi i ragazzi italiani?

5. Bisogna avere la patente per guidare un motorino in Italia?

6. Quanti anni ha Angela?

7. Quanti motorini vuole noleggiare Laura?

8. Quando bisogna pulire le candele?

9. Che cosa bisogna mettere nel motorino con la benzina?

10. Il proprietario garantisce i motorini?

B. Present tense (revision). ★

Complete the following sentences with the appropriate form of the <u>present tense</u> for the infinitive in brackets:

1. I ragazzi _____ (camminare) per le vie di Roma.
2. Giulia _____ (cercare) un distributore di benzina.
3. Scusa, Marco, perchè _____ (leggere) questo libro?
4. Giorgio non _____ (capire) come funziona il motorino.
5. I ragazzi _____ (dormire) alla Pensione Orlanda.
6. Tutti i meccanici _____ (garantire) la Vespa.
7. Noi _____ (preferire) il Boxer o il Ciao.
8. Scusi, signore, perchè non _____ (noleggiare) un'Alfa Romeo?
9. Se tu non _____ (andare) io non _____ (andare).
10. Ma ragazzi, _____ (essere) sempre stanchi e _____ (avere) sempre fame.

C. Volere and potere.

> | **Volere** | to want | **Potere** | to be able (can) |
> |---|---|---|---|
> | **voglio** | I want | **posso** | I can |
> | **vuoi** | you want | **puoi** | you can |
> | **vuole** | he, she, it wants | **può** | he, she, it can |
>
> ***vorrei** I would like :
> e.g. **Vorrei andare ma non posso.** I'd like to go but I can't.
>
> When you are talking about what you <u>want</u> or are <u>able to do</u>
> in Italian you use parts of **volere** and **potere** followed by the infinitive.
> e.g. **Vuoi venire?** Do you want to come?
>   **Anch'io voglio guidare.** I want to drive too.
>   **Non può camminare più.** He/she can't walk anymore.
>   **Posso noleggiare una macchina qui?** Can I (may I) hire a car here?
> **Vorrei** means <u>I would like.</u> It sounds a bit less blunt than **voglio** (<u>I want</u>)
> and for this reason it is commonly used in conversation.
> e.g. **Vorrei due litri di miscela.** I'd like 2 litres of two-stroke mixture.
>   **Vorrei vedere tutta Roma.** I'd like to see all of Rome.

Complete the following sentences by writing the appropriate form of <u>volere</u> or <u>potere</u>: ★

1. Gianfranco, _____ (volere) giocare a tennis o preferisci il calcio?

2. Mi dispiace, non _____ (potere) andare oggi, ho troppo lavoro.

3. Silvana _____ (volere) venire ma non _____ (potere).

4. Non _____ (volere) comprare il vestito perchè non mi piace.

5. Un momento, Marco, _____ (potere) venire qui?

6. Io _____ (volere) andare ma tu non _____ (volere).

D. Express the following in Italian: ★★

1. I want to go but I can't._____

2. He can't drive, he's only thirteen._____

3. Excuse me, sir, can you guarantee the scooter?_____

_____

4. But Miss, why do you want to hire a Ferrari?_____

_____

5. Do you want to play tennis today, Stefano?_____

_____

6. You can't eat all the rolls, Mario._____

_____

7. She doesn't want to clean the car._____

_____

8. I'd like to buy a new tyre, please._____

E.

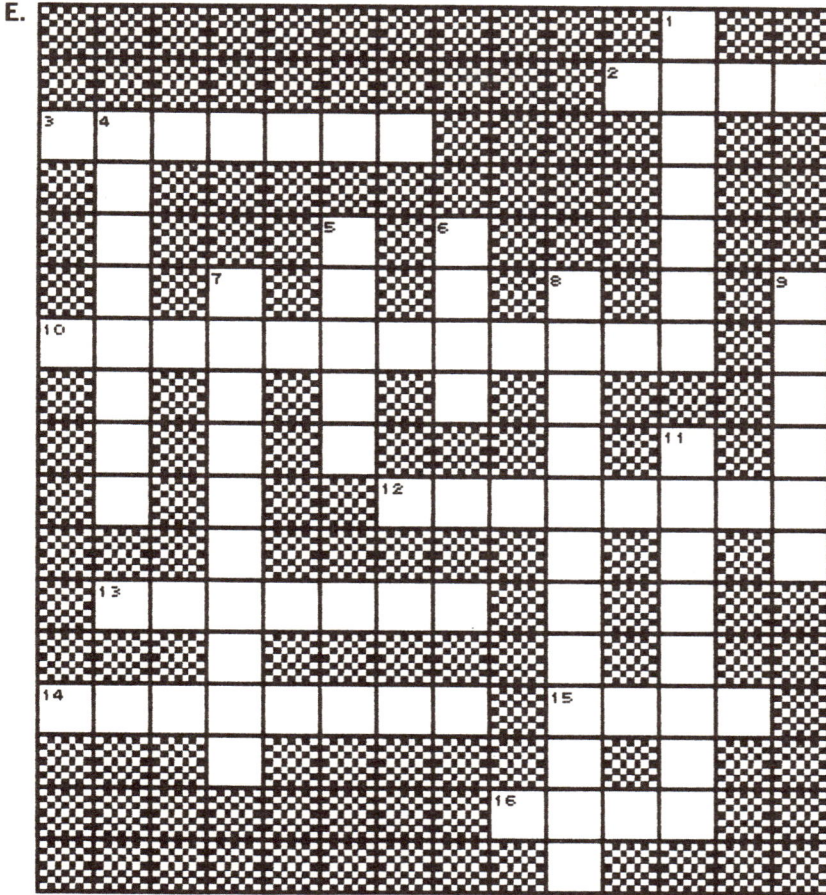

**Parole crociate –
motorini e macchine.**

Orizzontali

  2. Headlights
  3. Steering wheel
10. Accelerator
12. Traffic lights
13. Petrol
14. Car
15. Choke
16. Oil

Verticali

  1. Spark plugs
  4. Garage, workshop
  5. Brakes
  6. A make of
     motor scooters
  7. One-way (2 words)
  8. Luggage-rack
  9. Truck
11. Motor scooter

F. La macchina. Label this drawing in Italian: ★

il cambio

i fari

il paraurti
il cofano

il parabrezza

il serbatoio

G. Talking about the past – the perfect tense.

| Avere + | -are → -ato |
| | -ire → -ito |

Ho camminato per tre ore.	I (have) walked for three hours.
Ho dormito all'aeroporto.	I (have) slept at the airport.
Hai trovato l'orecchino, Anna?	Did you find the earring, Anna?
Ha capito la domanda, signore?	Have you understood the question, sir?
Abbiamo noleggiato il motorino.	We (have) hired the scooter.
Abbiamo garantito il motore.	We (have) guaranteed the motor.
Avete portato tutte le valige?	Did you carry all the cases?
Avete sentito questo motore?	Have you heard this motor?
Hanno visitato tutti i monumenti.	They('ve) visited all the monuments.
Hanno finito quella lettera?	Have they finished that letter?
	Did they finish that letter?

1. The *perfect tense* is used when an Italian speaker or writer wants to tell about things that (have) happened in the (not too distant) past.

2. To form the *perfect tense* in Italian you need two words.
   In most cases, the first word is a part of the verb **avere** (to have) and the second word is the *past participle* of the verb you want to put in the past.
   The **avere** part is called an *auxiliary* (helper) -
   it helps turn a *participle* into a *fully fledged verb.*
   How do you form the *past participle* of an **-are** verb?

   _____

   How do you form the past participle of an **-ire** verb?

   _____

   What happened to the **-ere** verbs?
   Keep your shirt on. We do them in the next chapter!

3. We have already seen that the Italian *present tense* can have at least two equivalents in English:

   e.g. **Mangiano all'aeroporto.** a) They eat at the airport.
   b) They are eating at the airport.

   Is there any difference in meaning between these two English *present tenses?* When would you use one rather than the other?

   _____

   _____

   What if we make a question of our Italian sentence:
   Mangiano all'aeroporto?
   What are the two English equivalents in this case?

   a)_____

   _____

   b)_____

   _____

What's all this talk about tense? That's how I feel when you start talking about it!

What are you worried about? *Tense* means <u>time</u>!

Similarly, there are two English equivalents for the Italian *perfect tense:*

Hanno mangiato all'aeroporto.
a) They have eaten at the airport.
b) They ate at the airport.

Is there any difference in meaning between these two English *past tenses?* When would you use one rather than the other?

_____

_____

_____

If we make it into a question what are two English equivalents?
Hanno mangiato all'aeroporto?

a)_____

b)_____

Never fall for the trap of trying to translate the English
<u>do</u> and <u>did</u> which often occur in questions.

e.g. Do you read Italian magazines?   **Leggi riviste italiane?**
     Did you walk much?   **Hai camminato molto?**

H. As you know, you need two words to form the perfect tense. Complete the following sentences by supplying the missing half of the verb. (In each case you will need the auxiliary: i.e. the appropriate part of <u>avere</u>): ★

☑ Ragazzi, ___*avete*___ trovato l'orecchino?

1. Noi non siamo stanchi perchè _____ noleggiato una macchina.

2. Antonio, _____ finito questa rivista?

3. Mi dispiace, non _____ capito la domanda.

4. Scusi, signore, _____ parlato con i carabinieri?

5. Ragazzi, è vero che _____ visitato il Colosseo?

6. Il proprietario _____ spiegato come funziona.

7. La signora Casati _____ preferito visitare un cugino.

8. I turisti tedeschi _____ visitato la Fontana di Trevi.

I. Parole nuove. Complete the following sentences by choosing one of the words from the list below: ★★

funziona
guidare
patente
deboli
rimanere
benzina
noleggiare

1. Non posso andare avanti. Voglio _____ qui.

2. Sono stanchi??? Questi ragazzi australiani sono _____

3. Per guidare basta avere quattordici anni; non bisogna avere la _____

4. Se hai paura di questo traffico posso _____ io.

5. Signorina, che tipo di motorino vuole _____?

6. Bisogna mettere _____ e olio insieme.

7. Dunque ragazzi, avete capito come _____ il motorino?

J. **Complete the following sentences using the appropriate form of the verb in the <u>perfect tense:</u>** ★

☑ Perchè volete camminare? Non _____*noleggiate*_____ (noleggiare) una Vespa?

1. Franco _____ (portare) i panini.

2. Signore, è vero che Lei _____ (aspettare) all'aeroporto per cinque ore?

3. Scusa, Marco, _____ (spiegare) il problema a Michelino?

4. Non parlo perchè non _____ (capire) la domanda.

5. Siete in ritardo perchè non _____ (sentire) l'altoparlante.

6. Ma guarda! Non hai finito: non _____ (pulire) le scarpe.

7. Tutti i carabinieri _____ (cercare) la bomba.

8. La signora Casati _____ (visitare) un cugino stamattina.

K. **Now that you have completed the sentences, translate them into English:** ★★

☑ Why do you want to walk? Aren't you going to hire a Vespa?

1. _____

2. _____

3. _____

4. _____

5. _____

6. _____

7. _____

8. _____

L. **A classmate passes you a note telling you that such and such is happening today (oggi). You know better. You pass back a note telling your friend that it happened yesterday (ieri).** ★★

☑ I giornalisti parlano con Karnitemova oggi.

I giornalisti hanno parlato con Karnitemova ieri.

1. Lorenzo noleggia un motorino oggi.

_____

2. Laura e Angela guidano per le vie di Roma oggi.

_____

3. La signora Paolucci chiama i carabinieri oggi.

_____

4. Piero pulisce la macchina oggi. _____

M. 1. **Which of these would you not put in your new Fiat?** ★★

l'olio   la miscela   la benzina   l'acqua

2. **Which of these is not operated by a pedal in front of the driver?**

il volante   i freni   l'acceleratore   la frizione

3. **Which of these would you be most unhappy to see on your car?**

la ruota   la gomma   la multa   la targa

4. **Which of these do the carabinieri use to identify your car?**

la patente   la targa   il volante   il motore

N. Are you ready to put some sentences into Italian? ★★★

1. I haven't found the petrol._____

2. Have you looked under the seat?_____

3. Yes, they understood the problem._____

4. Excuse me, sir, did you call the carabinieri?_____

5. We have waited for two hours and now we're leaving._____

6. Giorgio, Gino, why are you walking? Didn't you hire a scooter?_____

O. Bisogna, basta + infinitive.

> **Bisogna** means <u>it is necessary.</u>
> **Basta** means <u>it is enough.</u>
> Watch how they are used with *infinitives.*
> **Bisogna avere la patente?**
> Is it necessary to have a licence? i.e. Do you have to have a licence?
> **Basta parlare con il proprietario.**
> It is enough to speak to the proprietor. i.e. All you have to do is speak to the proprietor.

Express the following in Italian: ★★

1. Is it necessary to open all the suitcases?_____

2. No, it's enough to (i.e. it will do if we) open this case._____

3. Do you have to put (two stroke) mixture in this scooter?_____

4. No, all you have to do is put some petrol._____

5. Is it enough to see St. Peter's and the Colosseum?_____

6. No, you have to see everything._____

Suggested cultural background reading:
Regions of Italy, pages 46-49, Emilia-Romagna.

P. Il Calendario. ★★

Here are some important occasions in any year:

il Natale	Christmas
la Pasqua	Easter
la vacanza	the holiday(s)
il trimestre	the term
il mio compleanno	my birthday
il mio onomastico*	my name day

*This occasion is celebrated in Italy to mark the feast day of the saint whose name you share.

Write in Italian the day and date on which the following occasions fall during this year:

1. Il Natale _____

2. La domenica di Pasqua _____

3. Il mio compleanno _____

4. Il mio onomastico _____

5. Il Compleanno della Regina _____

6. Questo trimestre finisce _____

7. Il prossimo trimestre comincia _____

8. L'Anzac Day _____

Q. Buon viaggio e buon divertimento. ★

These expressions are typical of the Italian way of wishing people luck, success, enjoyment, etc., in whatever they are about to do. Italians express these good wishes regularly, as a matter of everyday courtesy - more often than we English speakers do.

Here are some more expressions. See if you can work out when they would be used: **buon appetito,** **buon lavoro, buon pranzo, buona fortuna, buon riposo, buona passeggiata.**

Note also:
Buon Natale	Happy Christmas
Buona Pasqua	Happy Easter
Buon Compleanno	Happy Birthday
Buon Anniversario	Happy Anniversary

Use the appropriate good wish as a caption for the drawings below:

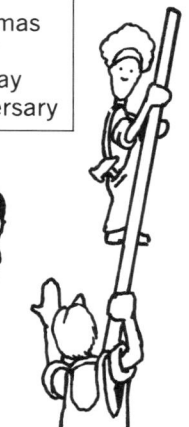

1. _____

2. _____

3. _____

4. _____

5. _____

6. _____

7. _____

8. _____

R. Question words + perfect tense.

Chi?	Who?	**Perchè?**	Why?
Che cosa?	What?	**Quanti/e?**	How many?
Dove?	Where?	**Quando?**	When?

Express the following questions in Italian: ★★★

1. Did you (pl.) play basketball?_____

2. Who drove the car?_____

3. Where did they hire the scooter?_____

4. What have you eaten today, Paola?_____

5. How many bread rolls did he eat?_____

6. When did we finish the match?_____

7. Why didn't I look for a bus?_____

8. How many tyres did she buy?_____

S. Talking about likes and dislikes.

mi piace	I like
ti piace	you like
non mi piace	I don't like
Ti piace Roma?	Do you like Rome?
Sì, mi piace molto.	Yes, I like it a lot.
Ti piace guidare?	Do you like to drive (driving)?
No, non mi piace guidare.	No, I don't like to drive (driving).

Don't forget the verb **preferire.** It's very handy for talking about your preferences.
e.g. **Sì, mi piace il Ciao ma preferisco la Vespa.**

If you really love something you can use the verb **amare** (to love).

e.g. **Ti piace la pasta?**	Do you like pasta?
Sì, mi piace moltissimo.	Yes, I like it a lot.
Amo lo sport.	I love sport.

Answer the following questions about your likes, dislikes and preferences: ★

1. Ti piace giocare a tennis o preferisci guardare?_____

2. Ti piace Roma?_____

3. Ti piace la scuola o preferisci rimanere a casa?_____

_____

4. Ti piace leggere?_____

5. Ti piace la Fiat "Uno"?_____

_____

6. Ti piace il motorino o preferisci la macchina?_____

_____

SCRIVIAMO

T.

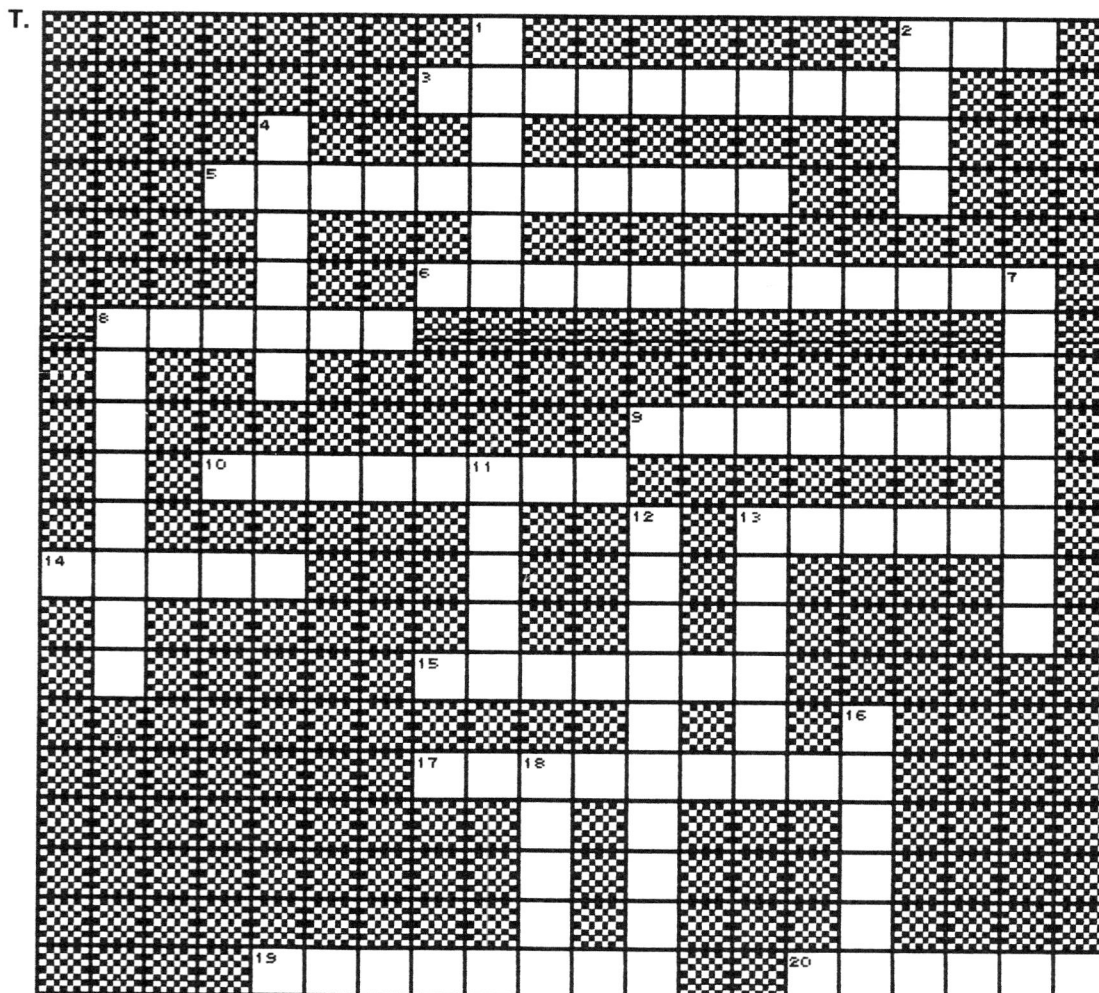

Parole crociate – rivisione.

Orizzontali
2. He can
3. We hire
5. Everywhere
6. Fun
8. I want
9. You (pl.) explain
10. Do you know that (3 words)
13. Well then
14. May I
15. I am walking
17. They do listen
19. It works
20. Near

Verticali
1. I'd like
2. Not much
4. Easy
7. Hospital
8. They want
11. City
12. Bike
13. Still
16. Non oggi
18. Of course!

U. Un po' di tutto. ★★★

If you can express the following in Italian without too many mistakes you have mastered Capitolo Cinque.

1. Why didn't you hire a scooter, Giuseppe? You don't have to have a licence.

2. I walked yesterday, I don't want to walk today.

3. I don't like driving through the streets of Rome.

4. If you're going to Rome, why don't you want to see the Colosseum?

5. I would like to buy an Alfa Romeo.

6. When did they finish this story?_____

7. Kevin's birthday is Sunday, the twenty-ninth of September. Happy birthday!_____

8. When can you explain how it works?_____

9. I can't guarantee the motor but there are four wheels._____

10. I have understood everything in this chapter._____

V. Componimento.   ★★★
See if you can make up a little dialogue in Italian. Try to follow the guidelines suggested below.
We'll call the characters Tizio and Caio but you're free to change the names if you like.

Tizio, calling around at Caio's place, greets his friend and asks him how he is.

T: _____

Caio replies that he's not very happy. He would like to go into town.

C: _____

Tizio says he doesn't want to go to town. He prefers to stay home.

T: _____

Caio asks what he wants to do at home.

C: _____

Tizio says he doesn't know.

T: _____

So Caio makes some suggestions: do you want to...

C: _____

Tizio replies that he did those things yesterday.

T: _____

So Caio makes more suggestions.

C: _____

Tizio doesn't like doing any of those things.

T: _____

Caio has had enough and says he's going into town.

C: _____

A. Motorini e macchine. ★★
Write vero or falso (true or false) after the following statements based on the Cultural Unit on pages 70 and 71 of the textbook, Motorini e macchine.

1. Molti giovani italiani vanno a scuola in motorino. _____

2. Bisogna avere la patente per guidare un motorino in Italia. _____

3. Quasi tutti i ragazzi italiani hanno un motorino perchè non costano molto. _____

4. L'età minima per guidare un motorino è sedici anni. _____

5. La velocità massima di un motorino è cinquanta chilometri all'ora. _____

6. In Italia è vietato portare passeggeri sui motorini piccoli. _____

7. Per comprare la miscela bisogna trovare un distributore di benzina. _____

8. Bisogna mettere la miscela sotto il sedile di una Vespa. _____

9. Se si ha bisogna di un meccanico bisogna cercare un'officina. _____

10. La grande fabbrica FIAT è a Milano. _____

11. Quasi tutti gli italiani hanno una Ferrari. _____

12. Le autostrade italiane sono veramente magnifiche. _____

13. Bisogna pagare per guidare sull'autostrada. _____

14. La velocità massima sull'autostrada è cento chilometri all'ora. _____

B. I segnali stradali. Write the following Italian expressions under the appropriate traffic sign:

senso unico   ponte mobile   divieto di svolta a destra
divieto di sosta   lavori in corso   divieto di svolta a sinistra
curva pericolosa a destra   bambini   parcheggio
curva pericolosa a sinistra

1. _____ 2. _____ 3. _____ 4. _____ 5. _____

6. _____ 7. _____ 8. _____ 9. _____ 10. _____

C. Si noleggiano motorini. Answer these questions in English: ★★★

1. On what day is the agency closed?_____

2. Their slogan is "Perchè camminare se puoi noleggiare?" What does it mean in English?_____

_____

3. What is P.zza Barberini? (It's near the scooter shop.)_____

4. If you had 280.000 lire, what would you hire and for how long?_____

5. Do you need a licence to hire a Vespa? Why?_____

_____

6. What would you pay if you hired a Ciao for two hours?_____

7. How much would you have to pay for a Suzuki 550 for a week in winter, and how much for a week in summer?

_____

8. How many people are you allowed on a Ciao?_____

TARIFFE

SCOOTERS FOR RENT

Roma Tel. 46.54.85
Via della Purificazione, 66
Vicino P.zza Barberini

AGENZIA BARBERINI
**APERTA DALLE 9.00 ALLE 19.30
DA MARTEDÌ A DOMENICA**

CONDIZIONI DI NOLEGGIO
- Noleggio minimo - un giorno
- La patente non è necessaria per motorini di 50 c.c.
- Nei mesi di giugno, luglio e agosoto:
  10% in più dei prezzi normali.
- Chilometraggio illimitato

TUTTI I MOTORINI SONO GARANTITI

GRUPPO	MODELLO	C.C.	POSTI	UN GIORNO	UNA SETTIMANA	DUE SETTIMANE	TRE SETTIMANE	UN MESE
A	Ciao Vespa	50	1	25.000	125.000	190.000	240.000	280.000
B	Boxer Si	50	1	25.000	125.000	190.000	240.000	280.000
C	Vespa	150	2	30.000	160.000	260.000	320.000	360.000
D	Honda	350	2	45.000	260.000	400.000	480.000	550.000
E	Honda	400	2	50.000	300.000	500.000	650.000	800.000
F	Suzuki 550 Honda CX	500	2	60.000	360.000	600.000	800.000	950.000

PERCHÈ CAMMINARE SE PUOI NOLEGGIARE?

CAPITOLO SEI
LA GITA TURISTICA

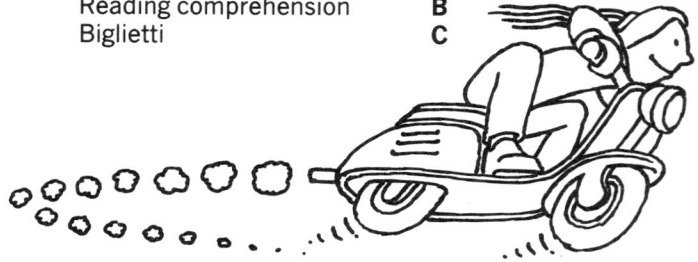

ASCOLTIAMO

A. Where are these people going? Listen carefully and circle the place you hear: ⭐

☺ il mercato	il tabaccaio	(l'albergo)	la banca	la questura
1. la piazza	il mercato	la banca	i giardini pubblici	il panificio
2. lo zoo	il parco	il negozio	il museo	il tabaccaio
3. l'ospedale	la piazza	il lago	l'aeroporto	la libreria
4. la libreria	l'ufficio informazioni	la lavasecco	la pasticceria	la piazza
5. i giardini pubblici	il grande magazzino	la pensione	la stazione	l'ufficio
6. il mare	l'agenzia	l'aeroporto	la metropolitana	la piscina
7. il banco	la banca	la chiesa	il cinema	il bar
8. la montagna	la metropolitana	la macelleria	il mercato	il museo
9. il panificio	la scuola	la sala giochi	lo stadio	il telefono pubblico
10. l'università	l'ufficio postale	la questura	la libreria	il negozio

B. Write down the list of things that Kevin is asking for: ⭐⭐

☺ _Una pianta della città. – A map of the city._

1. _____

2. _____

3. _____

4. _____

5. _____

6. _____

7. _____

8. _____

A. Domande sul fumetto. ⭐

1. Perchè non va a sinistra Laura?_____

_____

2. Laura va bene per il Colosseo?_____

3. Che cosa preferisce Faye?_____

4. Perchè Laura non può andare in quella direzione?_____

5. Quanti ragazzi vanno su un motorino?_____

6. Questo è vietato in Italia?_____

7. Dov'è la testa di Kevin?_____

8. Che cosa cerca Giorgio?_____

B. Volere + potere.

Volere to want	**Potere** to be able (can)
voglio	posso
vuoi	puoi
vuole	può
vogliamo	possiamo
volete	potete
vogliono	possono

Volere is the verb used to express *wish or desire.* Can you think of English words beginning with <u>vol</u>- which express

similar ideas?_____

_____

Potere is the verb used to express *ability* or *capacity.* Any English words beginning with <u>pot</u>- or <u>poss</u>- which express

similar ideas?_____

_____

Complete the following sentences by writing the correct form of <u>volere</u> or <u>potere</u>, then translate the sentence into English: ⭐

1. Non _____ (volere) vedere il Castel Sant'Angelo, sono troppo stanco.

_____

2. Ciccio non _____ (potere) guidare, ha solo tredici anni.

_____

3. Ragazzi, non _____ (potere) andare in quella direzione, è ''senso unico''.

_____

4. Chi _____ (volere) venire con noi?

_____

5. Questi turisti non _____ (potere) camminare più, _____ (volere) prendere l'autobus.

_____

6. _____ (vuole) mangiare adesso o preferisci aspettare un po'?

_____

C. Volere and potere. Express the following in Italian: ★★

1. Do you want to go to the pictures?

_____

2. I want to see the shops and the markets.

_____

3. Boys, do you want to drive or take the train?

_____

4. We want to stay here, we can't walk anymore.

_____

5. I would like to help but I can't.

_____

6. He can go but he doesn't want to.

_____

7. Gino, if you don't have a jumper you can't play.

_____

8. Excuse me, sir, but you can't drive in this direction.

_____

D. Expressing likes and dislikes.

If you are talking about liking one person, thing or activity you use **piace**.
If you are talking about liking more than one person, thing or activity use **piacciono**.
Study these examples:
Elena, ti piace questo vestito? Helen, do you like this dress?
Sì, mi piace moltissimo. Yes, I like it very much.
Mi piace Stefano, è così simpatico. I like Stephen, he's so cute.
Non mi piacciono tutte queste chiese. I don't like all these churches.
Mi piace guidare ma non mi piacciono questi autisti pazzi.
I like driving but I don't like these crazy motorists.

Ti piace Giorgio?

Choose one of the following expressions to complete the sentences below: ★★
...mi piace   ...ti piace   ...mi piacciono   ...ti piacciono
Then translate your completed sentence into English:

1. Lucio, _____ la nuova Fiat?

2. No, non _____ molto.

3. _____ Giovanna, è veramente simpatica.

4. Non _____ i monumenti, preferisco i negozi.

5. Guilia, _____ le fontane di Roma?

6. Se non _____ camminare puoi prendere l'autobus.

E. Give your opinion of the following. Use expressions like: non mi piace, mi piacciono, non mi piacciono. ★

Mi piace Laura.

1. _____
2. _____
3. _____
4. _____
5. _____
6. _____
7. _____
8. _____
9. _____

F. Respond to the following invitations according to your likes and dislikes: ★★

Vuoi camminare? *No, grazie, preferisco giocare.*

1. Vuoi andare al cinema? _____
2. Vuoi guardare la televisione? _____
3. Vuoi giocare a tennis? _____
4. Vuoi vedere i negozi? _____
5. Vuoi guidare? _____
6. Vuoi leggere i giornali? _____

G. Asking and giving directions. Looking at the map opposite, complete the following exercises:

1. a) Ask if there's a Post Office nearby.

   _____

   b) Answer:_____

   c) Ask how long it takes to walk there. _____

   d) Answer: _____

   _____

   e) Ask how to get there.

   _____

   f) Explain how to get there and exactly where it is.

   _____

2. a) Ask if there's a Chemist nearby.

   _____

   b) Answer:_____

   c) Ask how long it takes to walk there.

   _____

   d) Answer:_____

   e) Ask how to get there.

   _____

   f) Explain how to get there and exactly where it is.

   _____

   _____

   _____

3. You've just arrived in town and need to go to a particular place. Write a dialogue including the following:
   ☞ attracting someone's attention,
   ☞ saying why you want to go there,
   ☞ asking the best way of getting there.

   _____

   _____

   _____

   _____

   _____

LA CITTÀ di VILLANUOVA

Zoo

L'HOTEL   CAFFÈ   PIAZZA DANTE

STAZIONE CENTRALE

VIA RUGGERO SETTIMO

LA MACELLERIA BRUNI   LA PASTICCERIA

LA QUESTURA   IL TABACCAIO

VIALE   LIBERTÀ

L'UFFICIO POSTALE

LA SALA GIOCHI

IL GRANDE MAGAZZINO

IL SUPERMERCATO

CORSO   ITALIA

LA PENSIONE MARSALA

IL BAR NUOVO

LA PALESTRA

LA FARMACIA

IL CINEMA ROXY   ROXY

IL RISTORANTE

LA CLINICA

VIA   GARIBALDI

LA BANCA

IL CINEMA BARONE

VIALE   ROMA

LA BIBLIOTECA

IL MUSEO

L'UNIVERSITÀ

IL MERCATO

VIA   CAVOUR

LA CHIESA   STADIO COMUNALE   TU SEI QUI   L'OSPEDALE

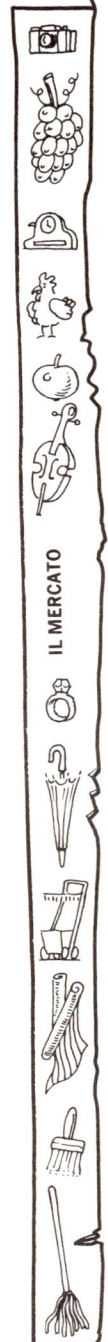

This map can be used for oral practice.   **LA PIANTA**

H. Express the following in Italian: ★★★

1. Do you like this shirt, Pina?

_____

2. I don't like waiting for the bus.

_____

3. I like the trains in Italy.

_____

4. Why don't you like Italian cars?

_____

5. Do you want to drive or do you like walking?

_____

6. I like tennis but I prefer basketball.

_____

I. Parole nuove. ★

1. At which one of these would you not spend the night?

   il campeggio   la macelleria   la pensione   l'albergo

2. Which won't be much help when you're hungry?

   la pasticceria   il generi alimentari   la biblioteca   la macelleria

3. Where won't you be going if you want some exercise?

   la palestra   la piscina   il panificio   lo stadio

4. Where will you phone if your house catches fire?

   lo zoo   l'università   il museo   i pompieri

5. Which is out of place?

   il magazzino   la chiesa   il mercato   il negozio

6. Which probably won't let you have a book?

   la sala giochi   la libreria   la biblioteca   la scuola

7. Which won't be much help when you're lost?

   il semaforo   la pianta   la questura   l'ufficio informazioni

8. Which figure would be the closest to the cost of a new Vespa?

   centocinquanta lire   novecentomila lire   mille lire   tremilaquattrocentocinquantacinque lire

J. Write the following in the plural (revision): ★

1. l'autista_____	5. il tipo_____	9. la nuvola_____
2. il bar_____	6. la via_____	10. il viaggio_____
3. la direzione_____	7. lo sport_____	11. l'acquedotto_____
4. la patente_____	8. il motore_____	12. il pomeriggio_____

Remember: nouns taken from English don't change in the plural: e.g. **l'hotel → gli hotel**

K. Write the following in the singular: ★★

1. Questi sedili sono molto comodi. _____

2. Questi autisti sono pazzi. _____

3. Le domande sono un po' esagerate. _____

4. Quelle domande sono facili. _____

5. I motori sono freddi. _____

6. I viaggi sono pericolosi. _____

7. I ragazzi sono così deboli. _____

8. Questi segnali sono proibiti. _____

L. a + the definite article.

> In Italian, when you say something like "I'm going to the museum", the words to + the join together.
> Look closely at these examples:
>
> **Vado al museo.**
> **Va all'ospedale.**
> **Andiamo allo stadio.**
> **Vado alla pasticceria.**
> **Vai all'albergo?**

Now complete this chart: ★

a + il = _____

a + l' = _____

a + lo = _____

a + la = _____

M. Write the correct form of a + definite article in front of the following, then give the English equivalent: ★

☆ _all'_ aeroporto _____

1. _____ albergo _____

2. _____ bar _____

3. _____ biblioteca _____

4. _____ cinema _____

5. _____ farmacia _____

6. _____ stadio _____

7. _____ edicola _____

8. _____ stazione _____

9. _____ ufficio _____

N. a + definite article, andare. Express the following in Italian: ★★

1. I'm going to the agency tomorrow. _____

2. Are you going to the lake? _____

3. Excuse me, Miss, are you going to the cake shop? _____

_____

4. Mrs. Vini is going to the hospital. _____

5. We're going to the zoo. _____

6. They go to the post office every day. _____

_____

O. Impersonal si.

> When Italians use **si** as the subject of a verb, they are not
> referring to anyone in particular but to people in general.
> Study these examples:
>
> **Si può giocare qui?** Can you/ May one/ Is it O.K. to play here?
> **Si mangia bene in questo ristorante.** You eat well/ One eats well/The food is good in this restaurant.
>
> The verb used with the impersonal subject **si** goes into the plural
> if the object is plural. This makes the **si** construction quite unique!
>
> Study this example:
>
> **In questo negozio si vendono riviste italiane.**
>
> | In this shop | they sell
are sold
one sells
you can buy | Italian magazines. |

Express the following in English: ★

1. Si parla italiano in questo negozio._____

2. Non si gioca a golf in questo campo._____

3. Scusi, si vendono i biglietti qui?_____

4. Si può fumare qui?_____

P. Answer the following questions in Italian using si as your subject: ★★

1. Si parla italiano in Svizzera?_____

2. Si gioca al calcio nel Colosseo?_____

3. Si può comprare una bibita vicino all'Altare della Patria?_____

   _____

4. Si noleggiano i motorini a Roma?_____

5. Si può vedere il Papa in Piazza San Pietro?_____

   _____

6. Si può comprare una nuova Fiat con centocinquantamila lire?_____

   _____

Q. Express the following in Italian: ★★

1. Do you catch the bus here?_____

2. Do you sleep well at this pensione?_____

   _____

3. Are bread rolls sold here?_____

4. Is it O.K. to photograph this zoo?_____

R. See if you can complete this summary of Chapters 5 and 6 by filling in the gaps: ✪✪

Mentre la signora Casati _____ (is visiting) un cugino i ragazzi _____

(visit) i monumenti importanti di Roma. Laura _____ (wants to see) tutto ma Giorgio e Dario

sono _____ (too tired). I ragazzi _____ (have walked) per tre ore.

Quando _____ (they see) i motorini che hanno i ragazzi italiani _____

(they want to hire) un motorino anche loro.

In Italia _____ (it's not necessary to have) la patente, basta

_____ (to be fourteen years old). Il signore _____ (explains)

come funziona il motore. I ragazzi mettono _____ (oil and petrol) e

_____ (they set off) come pazzi. I ragazzi _____ (are scared) perchè

le ragazze _____ (are driving) come veri autisti romani. Con l'aiuto di un tassista

_____ (they find) il Colosseo. Un carabiniere trova che gli australiani

_____ (do not understand) i segnali di traffico a Roma. Laura e Angela

_____ (explain) tutto e i ragazzi _____ (go home) alle sei di sera.

S. Parole crociate - ordinals. ✪✪

Orizzontali
2. **10th.**
5. **3rd.**
6. **1st.**
8. **5th.**
10. **8th.**
11. **32nd.**

Verticali
1. **6th.**
3. **4th.**
4. **2nd.**
7. **20th.**
9. **9th.**

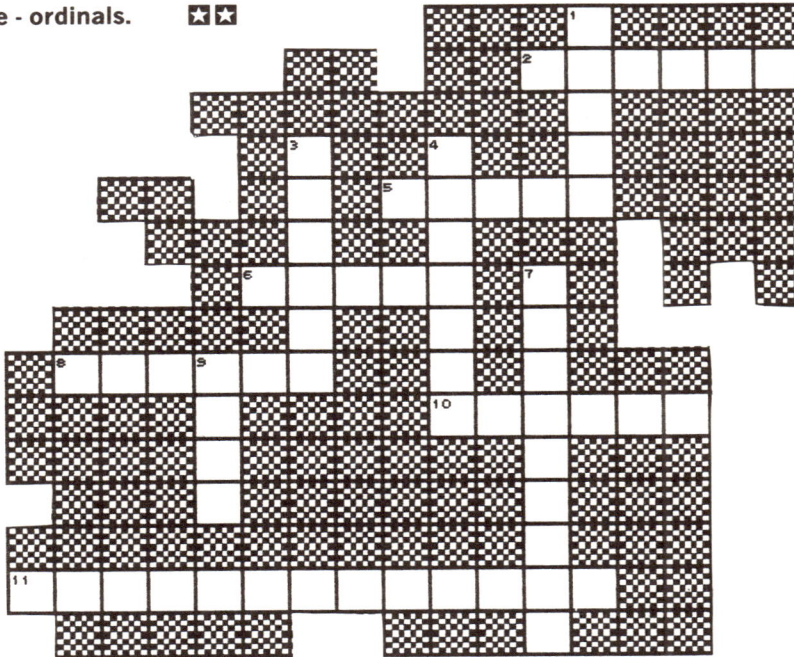

T. Maleducata.
We're still having trouble with <u>maleducati</u> who keep using the informal <u>tu</u> verb forms with people they ✪
really aren't all that familiar with, and Faye is the main offender. Kevin, always a stickler for correctness, has
been listening to her in Rome and at the end of the day presents her with a list of verbs she should have put into
the <u>Lei</u> form. What should she have said?

1. cammini_____   3. viaggi_____   5. spieghi_____

2. garantisci_____   4. vedi_____   6. rimani_____

U. Irregular nouns ending in -tà.

> There is a large number of nouns in Italian which ends in **-tà.**
> They correspond to English words that end in **-ty.**
> These words are *feminine* and *invariable* in the plural,
> i.e. the plural form of the word is the same as the singular.
>
> e.g. **l'autorità → le autorità**
>   **la città → le città**

Next to each of the following nouns write its English equivalent and its Italian plural form: ★

☺ la comunità   *the community*   *le comunità*

1. l'assurdità _____ _____

2. l'atrocità _____ _____

3. la difficoltà _____ _____

4. la personalità _____ _____

5. la qualità _____ _____

V. Now, see if you can work out the Italian words for the following: ★

1. poverty_____   4. maturity_____   7. humidity_____

2. speciality_____   5. purity_____   8. visibility_____

3. velocity_____   6. stupidity_____   9. hospitality_____

Il problema → i problemi. Don't worry about this one - just take note of it and learn it!!!

W.   **il portabagagli** - the luggage rack
i portabagagli - the luggage racks.
This is an example of a compound noun, i.e. one formed by joining two words together.
Can you see where the words have been joined in this case?
There are quite a few compound nouns formed with **porta:**
il portacenere   the ashtray
il portafogli   the wallet
il portalettere   the postman (more often called **il postino**)

Use the following word list to form compound nouns with porta.
Write the English meanings next to the nouns you form: ★★

☺ **il sapone**   the soap   *il portasapone*   *the soap-holder*

1. **i piatti**   the plates _____ _____

2. **gli spilli**   the pins _____ _____

3. **i sigari**   the cigars _____ _____

4. **la fortuna**   good luck _____ _____

5. **i cappelli**   the hats _____ _____

6. **i gioielli**   the jewels _____ _____

<u>Note:</u> These nouns are invariable in the plural.

X. Buono, buon, buona, buon'.
Look carefully at the examples of <u>buono</u> on page 87,7 of the textbook, then answer the following questions:
When <u>buono</u> is before a noun, it changes in the same way as the indefinite article (un, uno, una, un'). Write down

the rules for the use of <u>buono</u> before a noun:_____

_____

_____

How does <u>buono</u> vary if it's not before a noun?_____

_____

You're recommending certain places to a friend. Next to each drawing write the sentence suggested by each one: ★★

☑ Scuola professionale   2. Campeggio Tavolara   5. Ospedale Pubblico
☑ Banco di San Paolo   3. Trattoria Veronese   6. Agenzia Rossi
1. Aeroporto Leonardo da Vinci   4. Stadio Olimpico

☑ La Scuola Professionale è una buona scuola.

☑ Il banco di San Paolo è molto buono.

1._____

2._____

3._____

4._____

5._____

6._____

Y. | **San Pietro** - St. Peter's.
When Italians name a church they nearly always use the name of the saint who is the patron of the parish.
The Italian word for the saint is **il santo,** but before a name the word changes as follows:

San Pietro   Sant'Antonio   Santo Stefano
Santa Maria   Sant'Agata

What rules could you make about the way **Santo** changes?_____

_____

_____

_____

Write the correct Italian equivalent of Saint in front of the following: ★

1._____ Giuseppe   3._____ Andrea   5._____ Stefano

2._____ Agnese   4._____ Giovanni Battista   6._____ Cecilia

Z. Parole crociate - luoghi d'interesse.

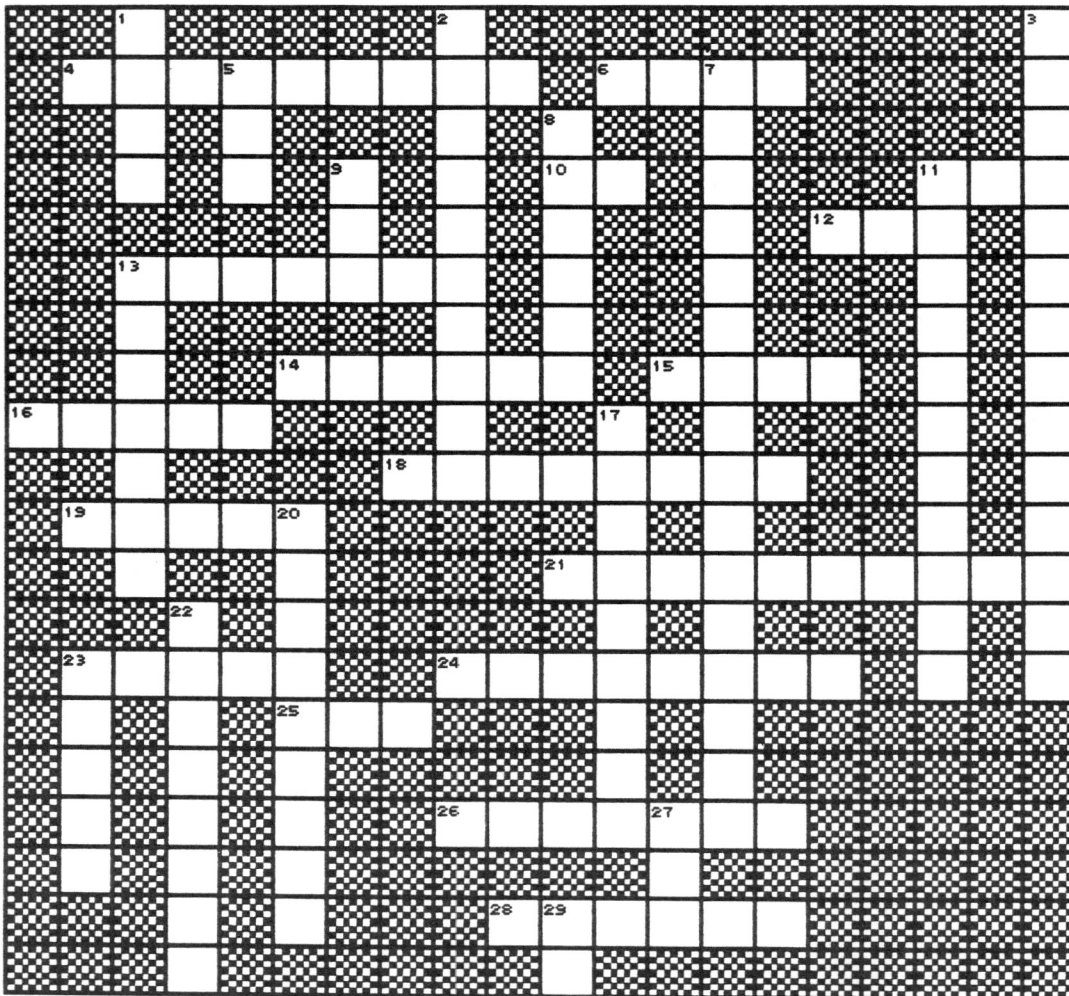

Orizzontali
- 4. Camp
- 6. Lake
- 10. Vado ... città.
- 11. Then
- 12. Street
- 13. Hotel
- 14. Church
- 15. Sea
- 16. Bank
- 18. Chemist's
- 19. City
- 21. Butcher's
- 23. Museum
- 24. Gym
- 25. Then
- 26. Shop
- 28. School

Verticali
- 1. Lake
- 2. Library
- 3. Post office
- 5. More
- 7. Grocer's
- 8. Picture theatre
- 9. Cafe
- 11. Cake shop
- 13. Agency
- 17. Dry cleaners
- 20. Airport
- 22. Hospital
- 23. Museum
- 27. Zoo
- 29. In città?
  No, non ... vado.

AA. How did they say...? ★★

1. Where is Laura going now? Why doesn't she go left?

_____

2. I'm going right because I want to find the Colosseum.

_____

3. Excuse me, sir, is this the way to the Colosseum?

_____

4. I don't like these ancient monuments.

_____

5. I don't like all these traffic signs.

_____

6. You're crazy, you can't drive like that!

_____

7. We didn't understand the sign.

_____

8. Here in Rome there are many crazy drivers.

_____

9. Please, is there a hospital around here?

_____

10. Ah, these Australians!

_____

BB. How would you say...? ★★★

1. Where are they going now? Why don't they go right?

_____

2. We're going left because we want to find St. Peter's.

_____

3. Excuse me, Miss, is this the way to the station?

_____

4. I don't like these scooters.

_____

5. I don't like all these crazy drivers.

_____

6. You're crazy, you can't go in this direction!

_____

7. I didn't understand the sign.

_____

8. Here in Rome there are many ancient monuments.

_____

9. Please, is there a chemist's around here?

_____

10. Ah, these Italians!

_____

CC. Un po' di tutto. ★★★

If you can express the following in Italian you can feel confident that you have mastered the material in Chapter 6. The letter in brackets refers to a Parliamo exercise which you should find helpful.

1. Why don't you ask if there's a post office near here? (A)

_____

2. O.K., I'll ask how to get to the supermarket. (B)

_____

3. Excuse me, madam, am I going the right way for the station? (C)

_____

4. I'll ask if the hotel is nearby or very far away. (D)

_____

5. He hasn't understood the traffic sign because he doesn't have a licence. (E)

_____

6. I've already looked at the map, but I can't find the zoo. (F)

_____

7. She wants to come to the city, but she can't. (I)

_____

8. I don't like these shops, they're too dear. (K)

_____

9. In this school you study (one studies) Italian, Spanish and English. (L)

_____

10. So you're going to St. Peter's Basilica. Have a nice trip! (H,J)

_____

DD. Componimento. ★★★

1. You've just moved house and you're sending out invitations to the house warming party. Most of your friends probably have a <u>pianta</u> but to be on the safe side you write clear directions how to get there. (An accompanying sketch map might help.) When giving directions, don't forget to make use of landmarks.

   e.g. **Quando arrivi a via Collins vedi un generi alimentari sulla destra.**
   Dopo il ponte c'è un campo sportivo...

_____

_____

_____

_____

_____

SCRIVIAMO

2. You've just received <u>una multa</u> from an unsympathetic <u>carabiniere</u>. You write to the <u>questura</u>, explaining what happened, giving your excuses and reasons why you can't pay the fine. ★★★

_____

_____

_____

_____

_____

_____

3. You've just opened a new <u>pensione</u> in Rome and you decide to draw up a list of regulations to be ★★★
   handed to each newly arrived guest.
   e.g. **In questa pensione non si gioca a pallone.**

_____

_____

_____

_____

_____

_____

_____

L'ITALIA OGGI

A. Roma.
   Write <u>vero</u> or <u>falso</u> after the following statements relating to the Cultural Unit, on pages 83-86 of the textbook:
   ★★

1. I giovani che cercano il Colosseo sono di Firenze. _____

2. Il Colosseo non è lontano, è molto vicino. _____

3. Per le partite di calcio di Serie A a Roma, bisogna andare allo stadio Olimpico. _____

4. Il ragazzo che guida il motorino senza mani è Giuseppe Manfredi, uno studente di suora Maddalena. _____

5. Si può comprare una bibita vicino all'Altare della Patria. _____

6. Si può vedere il Castel Sant'Angelo da San Pietro. _____

7. C'è un obelisco in mezzo a Piazza San Pietro. _____

8. Non ci sono molte fontane a Roma. _____

9. Il Papa parla in piazza quasi ogni domenica. _____

10. Al mercato di Porta Portese tutti i prezzi sono fissi. _____

11. Il mercato di Porta Portese è chiuso durante il weekend. _____

12. Molti ragazzi romani vanno al Gianicolo la domenica per vedere Pulcinella. _____

13. Le storie di Pulcinella piacciono moltissimo alle statue. _____

14. Antonio e l'altro ragazzo giocano per la Juve allo Stadio Olimpico. _____

15. La ragazza è in pericolo di perdere il braccio. _____

16. La signorina davanti alla fontana è molto timida e modesta. _____

17. Il conte Dracula vuole una bibita. _____

18. Mario vuole andare sul Treno degli Orrori. _____

19. Non ci sono canguri a Roma. _____

20. La signorina vicino a Piazza di Spagna non vuole prendere una multa. _____

B. You've been given a brochure on places to visit in Rome, but the explanations are all in Italian. ⭐⭐⭐
By doing some intelligent guess work, try to answer the following questions in English:

ALTARE DELLA PATRIA Piazza Venezia	Ultimato nel 1911 (G. Sacconi) per celebrare l'Unità d'Italia. Monumento a Vittorio Emanuele II. Conserva le spoglie del « Milite Ignoto ».	
ARCO DI COSTANTINO P.za del Colosseo	Costruito nel 315 per celebrare la vittoria su Massenzio a Ponte Milvio.	
BASILICA DI S. GIOVANNI	È la cattedrale di Roma. Fu fondata da papa Melchiade (311-314). La facciata principale è settecentesca. Nell'abside è conservato un prezioso mosaico del XIII sec.	
BIBLIOTECA NAZIONALE CENTRALE V.le Castro Pretorio	Nuovissima grandiosa sede della Bibl. Naz. inaugurata il 31-1-75, architetti Vitellozzi, Castellozzi, Dallanese. Possiede più di 2.500.000 tra volumi e opuscoli.	
CASA DI KEATS E SHELLEY P.za di Spagna, 26	Contiene cimeli e ritratti dei due poeti inglesi.	
CASTEL S. ANGELO O MAUSOLEO DI ADRIANO Lungotevere Castello	Costruito da Adriano (135-139) come tomba per sè ed i suoi successori; trasformato in fortificazione oggi ospita un museo artistico e militare.	
CATACOMBE di: Domitilla - Via delle 7 chiese, 282 Priscilla - Via Salaria Nuova, 430 S. Agnese - Via Nomentana, 349 S. Callisto - Via Appia Antica, 110 S. Sebastiano - Via Appia Antica, 132	Luoghi di rifugio e di preghiera; sepolture dei cristiani durante le persecuzioni; di solito ricche di affreschi e iscrizioni.	
COLOSSEO	È il più importante monumento della Roma antica. Eretto fra il 72 e l'81 dagli imperatori della famiglia Flavia, era destinato a pubblici spettacoli.	
FONTANA DI TREVI	La vasca è di Leon Battista Alberti (1453). Il disegno d'insieme delle sculture fra rocce e giochi d'acqua è opera di Nicola Salvi (1732-51). Nella nicchia centrale Oceano è trasportato su un cocchio da cavalli marini. È usanza gettare una moneta nella fontana per assicurarsi il ritorno a Roma.	
FORO ROMANO Via dei Fori Imperiali **PALATINO** Via S. Gregorio	Centro della vita pubblica di Roma antica. Resti di edifici pubblici e di lussuose ville private di epoca imperiale.	
GIANICOLO	Una delle colline di Roma con grande piazzale panoramico; al centro si erge il monumento a Garibaldi. Poco più avanti il monumento ad Anita Garibaldi.	

GIARDINO ZOOLOGICO Villa Borghese	Istituito nel 1911 e poi ampliato si estende su 12 ettari di un terreno, che cerca di ricreare un ambiente naturale per gli animali. All'interno si trovano il Museo di Zoologia e il Museo Africano.	
MUSEI VATICANI Viale Vaticano	Raccolta tra le più imponenti delle opere d'arte di tutti i secoli. Ne fanno parte i musei: Gregoriano Egizio, Pio Clementino, Chiaramonti, Collezioni d'Arte Religiosa Moderna, Gregoriano Etrusco, Gregoriano Profano, Pio Cristiano, Missionario Etnologico Storico; la Biblioteca Apostolica, le Gallerie delle Carte Geografiche, degli Arazzi, dei Candelabri, l'Appartamento Borgia, la Cappella Sistina, le Stanze e le Logge di Raffaello, la Cappella del Beato Angelico, la Sala dell'Immacolata e la Pinacoteca.	
PANTHEON Piazza della Rotonda H. 9-13; 14-17 D. 9-13; ⊖ L.	Eretto nel 27 a.C. da M. Agrippa, ricostruito al tempo di Adriano, consacrato al culto cristiano nel 606. Custodisce le tombe di Raffaello e dei Re d'Italia.	
PIAZZA DI SPAGNA e Trinità dei Monti	Centro romantico della Roma papale oggi cuore della più elegante zona commerciale di Roma. La chiesa di Trinità dei Monti, che la sovrasta, è collegata alla piazza dalla scenografica scalinata, originalissima realizzazione settecentesca.	
PORTA PORTESE	Aperta sotto Urbano VIII; vi si svolge ogni domenica mattina, nelle ampie strade circostanti, il « mercato delle pulci » di Roma.	
STADIO OLIMPICO Foro Italico	Detto anche « dei Centomila », fu inaugurato con una partita internazionale (Italia-Ungheria) e il 25 agosto 1960 vi si svolse l'inaugurazione della XVII Olimpiade.	
TERME DI CARACALLA Via delle Terme di Caracalla H. 9-16; D. e L. 9-13	Iniziate da Settimio Severo nel 206, inaugurate dal figlio Antonino Caracalla nel 217, funzionarono fino al VI sec. quando vennero distrutte dai Goti. Si ritiene che potessero essere utilizzate da 1600 bagnanti contemporaneamente. Vi si svolge la stagione operistica estiva.	
VIA APPIA ANTICA	La più importante delle strade consolari romane. Fu detta « regina viarum » per gli splendidi monumenti che sorgevano ai suoi lati. Sono tuttora visibili: la chiesetta del « Domine quo vadis », le Catacombe di S. Callisto e di San Sebastiano, gli avanzi del Circo di Massenzio e la Tomba di Cecilia Metella.	

1. When and why was the Altare Della Patria built?_____

_____

_____

2. Where is the Arco di Costantino situated?_____

_____

_____

3. What is the name of Rome's Cathedral? Who was the pope who founded it?_____

_____

_____

4. Where would you go to do some reading and research? (Give the Italian name and address)._____

_____

_____

5. Where did two famous English poets live?_____

_____

_____

6. Where is the Emperor Hadrian buried?_____

_____

7. Mrs. Casati visited some catacombs. (see exercise C) Name them and also the famous Roman road near which

they are situated._____

_____

_____

8. When was the Colosseum built? By whom was it built?_____

_____

_____

9. Who designed the Fountain of Trevi? Which custom is associated with this fountain?_____

_____

_____

10. What do you know about the Gianicolo?_____

_____

_____

CONTINUA

11. Where are Rafaello and the Kings of Italy buried? When and by whom was it built?_____

_____

_____

12. Where is the church of Trinità dei Monti situated?_____

_____

13. When is the market at Porta Portese open? How do you say flea market in Italian?_____

_____

14. Which is the most important road built in Roman times? Give Italian and English names._____

_____

C. **Mrs. Casati also did some sight seeing while she was in Rome. She collected all the tickets of places** ★★★
she visited and pasted them in her diary. Examine the tickets and write as much as you can about what she did.
Start your sentences with one of the following:

Sono andata...	I went...	**Ho mangiato...**	I ate...
Ho visto...	I saw...	**Ho preso...**	I took...

☑ Sono andata al Teatro Eliseo e ho visto _la commedia, Rugantino._

_____

_____

_____

_____

Teatro ELISEO
TE
Via Nazionale, 183 - Roma Tel. 46.21.14   Serie **F**
"RUGANTINO"
dot. **B**
Seconda Galleria
Fila   C   N.
MONTE DEI PASCHI DI SIENA
Graf-Roma S.r.l.

616555 A
MUSEI E GALLERIE
MONUMENTI   PONTIFICIE
L. 5000
MUSEI E GALLERIE
Tel. 06/7578757

PONTIFICIA COMMISSIONE
DI ARCHEOLOGIA SACRA
BIGLIETTO D'INGRESSO
ALLE CATACOMBE
DI S. SEBASTIANO
N° 48183

REV. FABBRICA
S. PIETRO
in VATICANO
CUPOLA
con
ASCENSORE
191455

POSTO UNICO
81624
S.I.A.E. - RM - BIMORPA-ROMA

TRATTORIA
« **Pierdonati** »
Roma - Via della Conciliazione, 39 - tel. 65.43.557
di **Garbati Carlo e Iole**
cod. Fisc. e Partita IVA 00624210589

Pane e coperto
Vino - Acqua
Pizze
Antipasti
Primi
Secondi
Contorni
Formaggi

Suggested cultural background reading:
Regions of Italy, pages 20-23, **Lazio.**

COSA DICIAMO?

ASCOLTIAMO

A. Which are the occupations that these people like? Circle the word you hear:

☑ autista	avvocato	dentista	idraulico	(astronauta)	maestro
1. autista	macellaio	marinaio	barbiere	panettiere	pittore
2. professore	postino	sarto	professoressa	poeta	scrittrice
3. astronauta	carabiniere	infermiera	parrucchiere	artista	autista
4. dottoressa	pittore	postino	poetessa	professore	programmatore
5. ciclista	farmacista	elettricista	autista	barbiere	avvocato
6. medico	postino	calzolaio	carabiniere	libraio	pompiere
7. frate	negoziante	idraulico	postino	barbiere	panettiere
8. farmacista	elettricista	bibliotecario	avvocatessa	dentista	professore
9. sarto	programmatore	primo ministro	calciatore	dottoressa	avvocato
10. parrucchiere	infermiere	barbiere	cameriere	orologiaio	alberghiere

B. Where do these people agree to meet? Write the place you hear:

☑ _Davanti al bar. — In front of the bar._

1. _____
2. _____
3. _____
4. _____
5. _____
6. _____

Now write when they will meet:

8. _____
9. _____
10. _____
11. _____
12. _____

A. Domande sul fumetto.

1. Secondo Dario, quando non dice bugie Giorgio?
_____

2. I ragazzi hanno passato una bella giornata?
_____

3. Hanno incontrato un carabiniere o un cameriere?
_____

4. Dove hanno visto una grande folla di tifosi?
_____

5. Hanno preso i mezzi pubblici o hanno noleggiato un motorino?
_____

6. Che cosa fa Giorgio?
_____

7. Quante cuccette ha prenotato la signora Casati?
_____

8. Secondo Laura, perchè Giorgio deve fare la dieta adesso?
_____

B. Dovere.

Volere to want	Dovere to have to	Potere to be able
voglio	devo	posso
vuoi	devi	puoi
vuole	deve	può
vogliamo	dobbiamo	possiamo
volete	dovete	potete
vogliono	devono	possono

It's easy to remember which is which: **dovere** for duty; **potere** for possibility; **volere** for *vot you vant.*

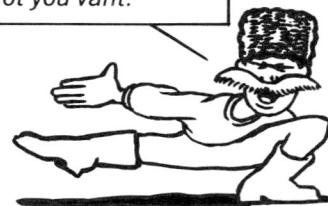

Dovere is used to express obligation, what one must or has to do.
Like volere and potere it is usually followed by an infinitive. What do the following sentences mean? ⭐

1. Devo andare adesso._____

2. Non devono fumare. È vietato._____

3. Non possiamo dormire. Dobbiamo fare le valige._____

4. Vogliono venire ma devono rimanere a casa._____

5. Se vuoi noleggiare un motorino devi avere quattordici anni._____

C. Complete the following by writing the appropriate form of <u>volere, dovere, potere</u>: ★

1. Scusi, signora, _____ (volere) prendere un antipasto?

2. Presto, Riccardo, _____ (dovere) ordinare adesso se hai fame.

3. Tonino non _____ (potere) guidare perchè non ha la patente.

4. Mi dispiace, noi non _____ (potere) venire, _____ (dovere) rimanere qui.

5. Non importa, ragazzi, non _____ (dovere) finire il pasto se non volete.

6. Che cosa _____ (volere) fare, Franca? _____ (potere) venire con noi?

D. Find how parts of <u>dovere</u> were used in the cartoon strip (pages 88-90 of the textbook) to express the following: ★★

1. Giorgio: We have to say something.

   _____

2. Casati: First we have to eat, then pack the cases.

   _____

3. Angela: Giorgio you musn't eat so much!

   _____

4. Laura: Yes, he must go on a diet now!

   _____

5. Giorgio: I don't have to go on a diet! Ridiculous!

   _____

E. Express the following in Italian: ★★★

1. I have to buy the meat._____

2. When do you have to catch the train, Marta?_____

   _____

3. He doesn't have to see every match._____

   _____

4. We must tell the truth!_____

5. Excuse me, Sir, you have to buy a ticket._____

   _____

6. You don't have to eat everything, boys._____

7. They have to find a post office._____

8. Does one have to book for this train?_____

   _____

F. Dovere, potere, volere. Express the following in Italian: ★★★

1. If you want to go to the disco you have to help.

_____

2. I would like to go but I haven't booked.

_____

3. He wants to become famous but he doesn't want to work.

_____

4. We must hurry. We have to catch the Milan train.

_____

5. They have to work, they can't come to the restaurant.

_____

G. Parole nuove. Che cosa ha fatto oggi? ★
Who would be most likely to give the following replies? Choose from the list of mestieri in the parole nuove on page 94 of the textbook and write the appropriate occupation in the space provided:

☺ Ho visitato la luna.   _l' astronauta_

1. Ho portato duemila lettere. _____

2. Ho finito il terzo capitolo. _____

3. Ho venduto sei chili di pomodori. _____

4. Ho lavorato all'ospedale. _____

5. Ho aiutato il medico. _____

6. Ho lavorato al ristorante. _____

7. Ho tagliato capelli, capelli, capelli. _____

8. Ho fatto due nuovi vestiti. _____

9. Ho guidato il taxi. _____

10. Ho arrestato un terrorista. _____

11. Ho aiutato i clienti in un negozio. _____

12. Ho giocato per l'Inter contro la Juve. _____

**H. Canzone ... I mestieri. Different people are telling you what they want to do with their lives.
You tell them what occupation they have to take up.** ★

Mi piace →
☺ Voglio —→ andare per il mondo. _Devi diventare marinaio._
Vorrei →

1. Mi piace stare e lavorare in campagna. _____

2. Vorrei andare sulla luna. _____

3. Voglio insegnare la matematica ai ragazzi._____

4. Vorrei combattere il dolore._____

5. Mi piace disegnare._____

6. Vorrei un mestiere pericoloso._____

7. Mi piacciono il teatro e il cinema._____

I. Parole crociate - i mestieri. ★★

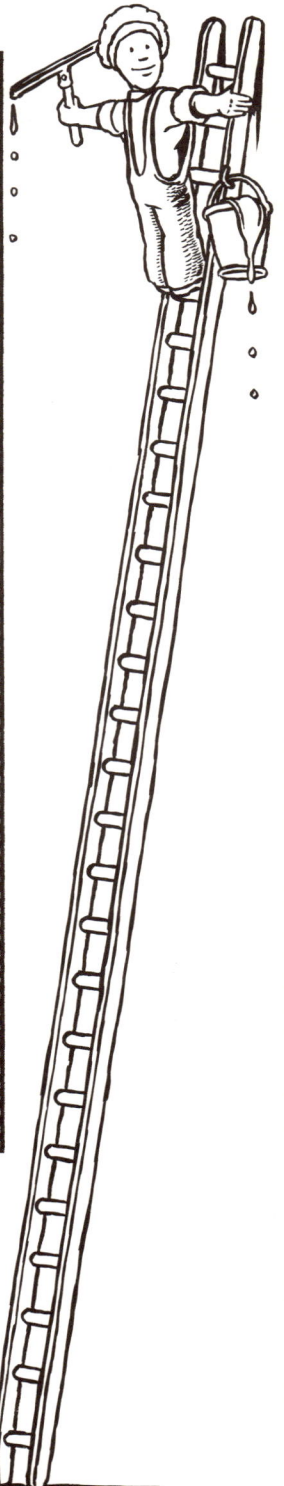

Orizzontali
1. Lavora con i computer
4. Lavora in campagna
7. Porta i piatti a tavola nel ristorante
9. Cucina in cucina
10. Guida tassì, autobus, ecc.
12. Portalettere
13. Artista
14. Taglia capelli
15. Lavora in ospedale

Verticali
1. Lei lavora a scuola
2. Il mestiere di Alessandro Volta
3. Vigile del fuoco
5. Prepara le medicine in farmacia
6. Lei ha studiato la legge
7. Vende e ripara le scarpe
8. Poliziotto
11. Prende la prima … a destra
13. Lavora in chiesa

J. Irregular verbs.

Essere	Avere	Andare	Sapere	Dire	Fare
sono	ho	vado	so	dico	faccio
sei	hai	vai	sai	dici	fai
è	ha	va	sa	dice	fa
siamo	abbiamo	andiamo	sappiamo	diciamo	facciamo
siete	avete	andate	sapete	dite	fate
sono	hanno	vanno	sanno	dicono	fanno

Translate the following into English: ★

1. Cosa diciamo alla signora Casati?_____

2. I ragazzi non sanno che è vietato fumare qui._____

_____

3. Cosa fai adesso? *Faccio le valige per il viaggio.*_____

_____

4. Giulio sa cosa fare ma non sa cosa dire._____

_____

5. Perchè non dici la verità? Sai che non devi dire bugie._____

_____

K. Complete the following sentences by writing the appropriate form of the present tense of the verb in brackets: ★★

1. Pigrone! Tu _____ (dormire) mentre io _____ (fare) tutto.

2. Chi _____ (sapere) perchè Martina _____ (dire) sempre bugie?

3. Paolo non _____ (capire) bene perchè non _____ (ascoltare).

4. Ma Gina, perchè non _____ (fare) un po' di lavoro?

5. Se Aldo _____ (finire) stamattina _____ (partire) alle sei.

6. Se Mario non _____ (sapere) dov'è la pensione _____ (potere) domandare.

7. Ragazzi, che cosa _____ (fare) di bello domenica?

8. Emilio e Luisa non _____ (dire) niente perchè non _____ (sapere) niente.

L. Irregular verbs. Complete the following chart: ★

	Essere	Avere	Andare	Sapere	Dire	Fare
io	sono					
tu		hai				
lui/lei			va			
noi				sappiamo		
voi					dite	
loro						fanno

M. Express the following in Italian: ★ ★ ★

1. I do everything in this house.

_____

2. What are you saying, Pina?

_____

3. Excuse me, Miss, are you going to Naples?

_____

4. We're not hungry, we're thirsty!

_____

5. You are good, boys, but you're not perfect.

_____

6. Emilia, do you know when the train leaves?

_____

7. What is the loudspeaker saying?

_____

8. Let's pack (do) the cases tomorrow.

_____

N. Dire, sapere, fare.
How were parts of <u>dire, sapere</u> and <u>fare</u> used to express the following in the cartoon script? ★ ★

1. What'll we do? If we say we hired scooters we're in trouble.

_____

2. You (pl.) know what Mrs. Casati is like.

_____

3. I'm sorry but I always tell the truth, I don't like telling lies.

_____

4. The only time Giorgio doesn't tell lies is when he's sleeping.

_____

5. Let's say we took the bus.

_____

6. Giorgio, what are you doing? ....What are you saying?

_____

7. The others are telling the truth._____

O. Past participles of -ere verbs.

> You will remember that the *past participle* is the *second half* of the perfect tense, e.g. **abbiamo camminato:** we (have) walked.
>
> The regular pattern for forming past participles is:
>
> **-are** → -ato e.g. **noleggiare → noleggiato**
> **-ere** → -uto e.g. **credere** → **creduto**
> **-ire** → -ito e.g. **dormire** → **dormito**
>
> So there is a regular past participle ending for **-ere** verbs, i.e. **-uto:**
> e.g. **avere → avuto, sapere → saputo, vendere → venduto**
>
> But more often than not **-ere** verbs have their own individualised, custom-made past participle. This means that you have to learn them, but they are so common that you soon get used to them.
>
> Here are some of the most important irregular past participles:
>
> | | | | |
> |---|---|---|---|
> | **vedere** | → **visto** | **chiudere** | → **chiuso** |
> | **leggere** | → **letto** | **decidere** | → **deciso** |
> | **mettere** | → **messo** | **perdere** | → **perso** |
> | **prendere** | → **preso** | **dire** | → **detto** |
> | **scrivere** | → **scritto** | **fare** | → **fatto** |
>
> ☛ **Fare** and **dire** are really **-ere** verbs in disguise.
>   They have evolved from early Italian forms, **facere** and **dicere**.
>
> ☛ **Vedere** and **perdere** also have regular past participles, **veduto** and **perduto**.
>
> ☛ The past participle of **aprire** is **aperto**.
>
> ☛ Can you work out what this expression means?
>
> **Detto, fatto!** _____

Present → perfect tense. ★★
Change the following sentences from statements or questions about <u>the present</u> to statements or questions about <u>the past.</u> You do this by changing the verb into <u>the pefect tense.</u> (Remember you'll need two words).

☺ Stefano cammina tutta la mattina.

Stefano ha camminato tutta la mattina.

1. Mimmo e Bianca noleggiano una macchina per tre giorni.

_____

2. Sì, capiamo, perchè spiega tutto così bene.

_____

3. Chi crede a questa storia ridicola?

_____

4. Perchè leggi tutti questi giornali?

_____

5. Dove mettete i biglietti per il pullman?

_____

6. Signor Barca, perchè non prende l'autobus?

_____

7. Cesarino prenota quattro cuccette.

_____

8. Che cosa fai, Faye? Dormi tutto il giorno?

_____

9. Perchè non aprite una finestra?

_____

10. Chiudono l'aeroporto durante il temporale.

_____

P. Now translate your <u>perfect tense</u> sentences into English: ★

1._____

2._____

3._____

4._____

5._____

6._____

7._____

8._____

9._____

10._____

Q. Parole nuove. ★
Complete the following sentences by choosing the appropriate word from the accompanying list:

fuoco   nuotare

folla

pigrone   carne

cuccetta

pomeriggio

biglietto

tagliare

diventare

1. Ho prenotato una _____ perchè mi piace dormire durante il viaggio.

2. La _____ che vende questo macellaio è molto cara.

3. Se vuoi combattere il dolore devi _____ medico.

4. Ci sono molti tifosi allo stadio?   Sì, c'è una grande _____

5. Ecco i pompieri, ma dov'è il _____ ?

6. Non posso andare, devo _____ l'erba.

7. Devo lavorare domani mattina. Posso venire durante il _____ ?

8. Se vuoi prendere il treno devi comprare un _____

9. No, non vado in piscina, non mi piace _____

10. Tu non hai fatto niente oggi! _____ !!

R. Change the following sentences from the <u>perfect</u> to the <u>present tense</u>: ★★

★ Giorgio ha mangiato un po' troppo. _Giorgio mangia un po' Troppo._

1. La signora Vavallo ha passato una bella giornata a Roma._____

_____

2. Ho messo la valigia sopra il banco._____

3. Hai sentito l'altoparlante?_____

4. Signor Pappalardo, perchè non ha aperto la lettera?_____

_____

5. Scemo, hai perso tutto!_____

6. La signora Casati ha saputo che Angela ha guidato un motorino._____

_____

7. Antea e Simone hanno avuto molti problemi._____

_____

8. Abbiamo chiuso l'edicola alle sette di sera._____

_____

9. Sono sicuro che avete detto la verità._____

_____

10. Non ho fatto molto sabato sera._____

S. Conoscere. ★

> **Conoscere,** <u>to know (a person or place)</u>, is not an irregular verb, because its endings follow the normal **-ere** verb endings.
> But you do have to be careful with the way you pronounce it:
> **-sc-** in Italian can be pronounced like the English **sk** or **sh**.

Suggested cultural background reading: Regions of Italy pages 50-53, Abruzzo.

Complete this table indicating also the correct pronunciation of each person.

	Conoscere	sk / sh
io	conosco	sk
tu		
lui		
lei		
Lei		
noi	conosciamo	sh
voi		
loro		

T. Sapere and conoscere.

> **Sapere** and **conoscere** both mean to know, but in quite different senses.
>
> **Sapere** means to know a fact, to know that something is true.
>
> Where it has this meaning **sapere** is followed by **che**:
>
> e.g. **Sai che non bisogna avere la patente per un motorino?**
>   Do you know that you don't have to have a licence for a scooter?
>
> When **sapere** is followed by an *infinitive* it means to know how to do something:
>
> e.g. **So guidare una Vespa.**
>   I know how to drive a Vespa.
>
> In the *perfect tense*, **sapere** can mean to find out, to hear about:
>
> e.g. **La signora Casati ha saputo che i ragazzi hanno noleggiato i motorini.**
>   Mrs. Casati found out that the kids hired the scooters.
>
> **Conoscere** usually means to be acquainted with a person or a place:
>
> e.g. **Conosciamo Giorgio.**
>   We know (are acquainted with) Giorgio.
>
> **Conoscete bene Roma?**   Do you know Rome well?
>   Are you well acquainted with Rome?

Express the following in English: ★

1. Non puoi venire in piscina perchè non sai nuotare.

_____

2. Scusi, signore, sa dov'è la stazione?

_____

3. Non sapete che hanno chiuso il mercato?

_____

4. Certo che questa carne è buona. Conosco il macellaio!

_____

5. Ho conosciuto una ragazza molto simpatica alla spiaggia.

_____

6. Come hai saputo che conosco Caterina?

_____

7. So guidare ma non posso. Ho solo tredici anni.

_____

8. Conosco bene questa città ma non so se c'è un medico qui vicino.

_____

U. I mestieri.
For each drawing, write the name of the occupation and the shop related to it. To help you, here is the list of occupations: farmacista, macellaio, direttore, tabaccaio, commessa, medico, bibliotecaria, professore.

1. La commessa.
   Il negozio.

2. _____

   _____

3. _____

   _____

4. _____

   _____

6. _____

5. _____

   _____

8. _____

   _____

7. _____

   _____

V. How did they say...? ★★

1. What'll we do?_____

2. We have to say something._____

3. Let's say we took the bus._____

4. We saw so many interesting things._____

5. We met a very nice policeman._____

6. Did you see all these places in just one day?_____

_____

W. How would you say...? ★★★

1. What'll we say?_____

2. We have to do something._____

3. Let's catch the bus._____

4. We did so many interesting things._____

5. They met a very unpleasant waiter._____

6. I saw all these places in just two days._____

X. Un po' di tutto.
If you can express the following in Italian you can feel confident that you have mastered the material in Chapter 7. The letter in brackets refers to a Parliamo exercise which you should find helpful.

1. No, I didn't walk, I caught the bus. (A)

_____

2. We say so many interesting things. (B)

_____

3. Let's go to the Colosseum; it's near here. (C)

_____

4. I didn't tell a lie, I told the truth! (D)

_____

5. The train leaves at a quarter past eleven. (E)

_____

6. The bus arrives at 10 p.m. (F)

_____

7. They have to finish in sixth place. (G)

_____

8. I don't know if there is a police station around here, but there's a policeman. (H)

_____

9. I want to buy a bandaid but I can't find a chemist. (I)

_____

10. The hospital? Of course they know where it is! (L)

_____

Y. Componimento. ★★★

1.A friend has written from the country trying to arrange a day in town with you.
  Write back saying that you can't go at the time he/she suggested because you have to ... (you'll think of a
  reason). You then suggest another time and a place where you can meet:

_____

_____

_____

_____

_____

_____

_____

_____

2.Your Italian teacher has taken you for a week's excursion to Rome. Your mum is expecting a letter full of news.
  You've only time for a postcard but make sure you tell her what you've been doing, what you've seen, what
  sort of transport you used, who you met, etc:

_____

_____

_____

_____

_____

_____

_____

_____

3.Write a dialogue in which two people arrange to go out together. You will find it helpful to look at page 98
  of the textbook. Once you have the idea, try to write it without looking at the textbook:

_____

_____

_____

_____

_____

_____

_____

_____

_____

A. Negozi e alberghi.
  Write answers to these questions referring to the photographs in the Cultural Unit, on pages 96-97 of the textbook:

1. Voglio giocare a calcio. Dove vado?

   _____

2. Vorrei comprare delle scarpe e un vestito. Dove vado per trovare i negozi?

   _____

3. Voglio imbucare una cartolina. C'è un ufficio postale qui vicino?

   _____

4. Ho avuto un piccolo incidente stradale. Mi fa male il braccio. Dove posso andare?

   _____

5. Vado bene per il municipio?

   _____

6. Scusi, e per i vigili urbani?

   _____

7. Vedo che l'Oasi è un ristorante - pizzeria. Ma che cos'è il Moderno?

   _____

8. Dove vado per comprare cartoline, francobolli e carta da lettere?

   _____

9. Dove si vende il sale?

   _____

10. L'albergo costa di più o di meno della pensione?

    _____

11. Se una pasticceria non vende la pasta dove si va per comprare gli spaghetti?

    _____

12. Che cosa sono Epoca, Gente, Amica e Oggi?

    _____

B. The **pensione** is a cheaper alternative to the **albergo** (hotel). Many budget-conscious tourists prefer the pensione which is usually run as a family business, thus providing the more informal atmosphere not always available in classier establishments. (Many return from their trip to Italy with stories about how they were made to feel part of the family in a favourite pensione.)

In the big tourist towns the pensioni cluster around the station in particular - a fact appreciated by tired train travellers. In Rome there must be hundreds in the streets surrounding the main railway station, Stazione Termini. You will often find several pensioni in the one building. To compare what they have to offer, take the creaking old lift from floor to floor and ring some front door bells!

Below is a list of services offered by top hotels. Next to each one write if you think a normal pensione would offer that service: Credo di sì. I think so.
Credo di no. I don't think so.

Ascensore	*Credo di sì.*
Bar	
Ristorante	
Parcheggio custodito	
Auto alla stazione	
Spiaggia privata	
Parco o giardino dell'esercizio	
Accessibile agli handicappati	

Gabinetto privato	
Camerini per bagni o fanghi	
Apparecchio radio	
Aria condizionata	
Telefono urbano	
Apparecchio TV	
Acqua corrente fredda	
Acqua corrente calda e fredda	

C.

Che lavoro ti piacerebbe fare? What work would you like to do?	**Mi piacerebbe ...** I'd like to ...	**Vorrei ...** I'd like to ...
Che lavoro fanno tua mamma e tuo papà? What work do your mum and dad do?		

A recent newspaper survey asked students at a liceo scientifico in Bologna what work they would like to do when they leave school and what work their parents do. Here are a few replies:

Giuliana Abbati: Voglio fare l'hostess o la segretaria. Mio padre è impiegato dell'Air Italia e mia madre è casalinga.
Matteo Ercolani: Se posso, voglio fare l'attore. Ma so che è molto difficile. Mio padre è idraulico e mia madre fa la sarta.

Lucrezia Valsecchi: I bambini mi piacciono molto. Ho due sorelline. E così dico sempre che vorrei fare la maestra. Ma non sono ancora sicura. Mio padre è direttore di una banca e mia madre vuole lavorare ma non può perchè deve badare alle due bambine.

Interview two of your friends (in Italian of course) and write down their answers:

a)

b)

CAPITOLO OTTO
ALLA TRATTORIA

ASCOLTIAMO

A. Which course on the menu is being ordered? Is it <u>antipasto, primo, secondo, contorno o dolce?</u>
Circle the appropriate one:

☺ Antipasto   Primo   (Secondo)   Contorno   Dolce

1. Antipasto   Primo   Secondo   Contorno   Dolce

2. Antipasto   Primo   Secondo   Contorno   Dolce

3. Antipasto   Primo   Secondo   Contorno   Dolce

4. Antipasto   Primo   Secondo   Contorno   Dolce

5. Antipasto   Primo   Secondo   Contorno   Dolce

6. Antipasto   Primo   Secondo   Contorno   Dolce

7. Antipasto   Primo   Secondo   Contorno   Dolce

8. Antipasto   Primo   Secondo   Contorno   Dolce

9. Antipasto   Primo   Secondo   Contorno   Dolce

10. Antipasto   Primo   Secondo   Contorno   Dolce

B. Write down the word that was used to describe the meal:
Was it ottimo/a, squisito/a, buonissimo/a, così così, pessimo/a?

☺ _squisita_

1. _____

2. _____

3. _____

4. _____

5. _____

6. _____

7. _____

8. _____

9. _____

10. _____

A. Domande sul fumetto.

1. In quanti sono la signora Casati ed i ragazzi?

_____

2. La tavola è pronta? Che cosa deve fare il cameriere?

_____

3. Che cosa hanno di buono come antipasto?

_____

4. Che cosa suggerisce il cameriere per il primo?

_____

5. Che cosa ha preso Angela per il secondo?

_____

6. Che cosa fa il cameriere tutto il giorno?

_____

7. Che cosa vogliono mangiare i ragazzi insieme alla carne?

_____

8. Perchè Giorgio dice che i panini sono dagli scavi di Pompei?

_____

9. Perchè non prendono un po' di acqua minerale?

_____

10. A che ora parte il treno per Catania?

_____

B. Irregular Verbs. Complete the following table: ★

	sapere	dire	fare	bere	venire	andare
io	so					
tu		dici				
lui/lei			fa			
noi				beviamo		
voi					venite	
loro						vanno

C. Express the following in Italian: ★ ★

1. Do you know that Pino is coming?

_____

2. You can come, Gina, but you musn't drink the wine.

_____

3. If they come, I'm not going.

_____

4. Gina, Franco, what are you doing? Why don't you come to Capri?

_____

5. I'm not drinking much because I'm not thirsty.

_____

6. They say you're not coming, Mimmo. Is it true?

_____

D. Parole crociate - irregular verbs. ★

Orizzontali
2. You have (sing.)
3. We know
6. I do
8. You say (pl.)
10. They come
11. You come (pl.)
12. You drink (pl.)
14. You go (Lei)
17. He can
18. I know
19. She speaks
20. They are, I am
21. They can
22. We have
23. I tell
24. They do

Verticali
1. They say
2. I have
4. You are (pl.)
5. She tells
6. He does
7. You make (sing.)
8. We must
9. I drink
11. I come
13. I want
15. I sleep
16. I finish
17. We can

SCRIVIAMO

E. La lettera di Giorgio. ★★
From Giorgio's letter to his mother choose five statements which you consider to be untrue:
a) Write the statement in Italian.
b) Translate it into English.
c) Explain why you would challenge it.

☑ a) Dalla finestra al secondo piano posso vedere tutta la città: San Pietro, il Colosseo, la Via Veneto, le Catacombe...

☑ b) From the window on the second floor I can see the whole city: St. Peter's, the Colosseum, Via Veneto, the Catacombs...

☑ c) You couldn't possibly see all these things from a second floor window. They are all in different parts of Rome. The Catacombs are underground.

1. a)_____
   b)_____
   c)_____
2. a)_____
   b)_____
   c)_____
3. a)_____
   b)_____
   c)_____
4. a)_____
   b)_____
   c)_____
5. a)_____
   b)_____
   c)_____

F. Parole nuove. ★

1. Which of these won't you find on a Pizza Capricciosa?
   il prosciutto   il formaggio   i funghi   i fagioli   _____
2. Which of these is not a condimento?
   l'aceto   il riso   l'olio   il pepe   _____
3. Which is the odd one out?
   la trattoria   l'osteria   la tavola calda   la macelleria   _____
4. Which one doesn't belong?
   al burro   al cinema   alle vongole   alla carbonara   _____
5. Which of these is not a contorno?
   le patatine   i fagioli   l'insalata mista   il sugo   _____
6. Which one is not a vegetable?
   la lattuga   l'anguria   la cipolla   il cavolo   _____
7. Which one is not a fruit?
   la ciliegia   la fragola   l'albicocca   il cetriolo   _____

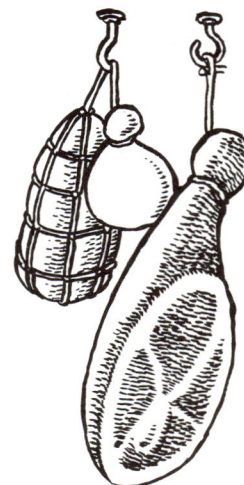

8. Which is the odd one out?

mezzo chilo   cinque etti   cinquanta grammi   cinquecento grammi   _____

9. Which is not an antipasto?

frutti di mare   prosciutto e melone   lasagne al forno   peperoni ripieni   _____

10. Which wouldn't you serve to a vegetarian?

spaghetti alla napoletana   spaghetti alla carbonara   pasta e fagioli   fettuccine   _____

11. Which would make the most unusual primo?

zuppa di pesce   zuppa inglese   zuppa di verdura   brodo di manzo   _____

12. Which would you serve someone who can't stand veal?

calamari fritti   saltimbocca alla romana   cotoletta   scaloppine al vino   _____

13. Which is not used for eating?

il bicchiere   il cucchiaio   il coltello   la forchetta   _____

14. Which verb doesn't believe in taking -isc-?

digerire   gradire   suggerire   partire   pulire   _____

G. Il menù.   ⭐

It's your birthday and you're being taken to an Italian restaurant where you're allowed to have anything you like. You're hungry, so pick something from each course. Write your choice below:

Antipasto _____

Primo _____

Secondo _____

Contorno _____

Dolce _____

Bevanda _____

H. You've just got a holiday job in an Italian restaurant as a waiter/waitress.   ⭐⭐⭐

You have to rehearse some handy expressions waiters/waitresses need to know. How will you say...

1. What would you like, Sir? _____

2. How many of you are there? _____

3. Just a moment while I clean this table. _____

4. What will you have as a main course? _____

5. The cook's speciality is roast chicken. _____

6. The entrees are nearly ready. _____

7. Today I suggest the strawberries. _____

8. Enjoy the meal, everybody! _____

9. Is everything alright? _____

10. Here's the bill, Miss. _____

11. No, we don't take American Express. _____

I. Parole crociate - al ristorante.

Orizzontali
1. Entree
3. Cooked the hunter's way
8. Tagliatelle
9. A popular antipasto (3 words)
11. Fruit salad
12. Always on the table next to olio
15. Cake
16. Hors d'oeuvre
18. A cheap place to get a meal (2 words)

Verticali
1. You might choose this for your primo (3 words)
2. Un condimento
4. Palle di carne
5. Bianco o rosso?
6. Steak
7. A cola drink
10. Un sugo con uova e prosciutto
13. Una cotoletta ... milanese
14. You'll find it next to aceto
17. Un altro condimento

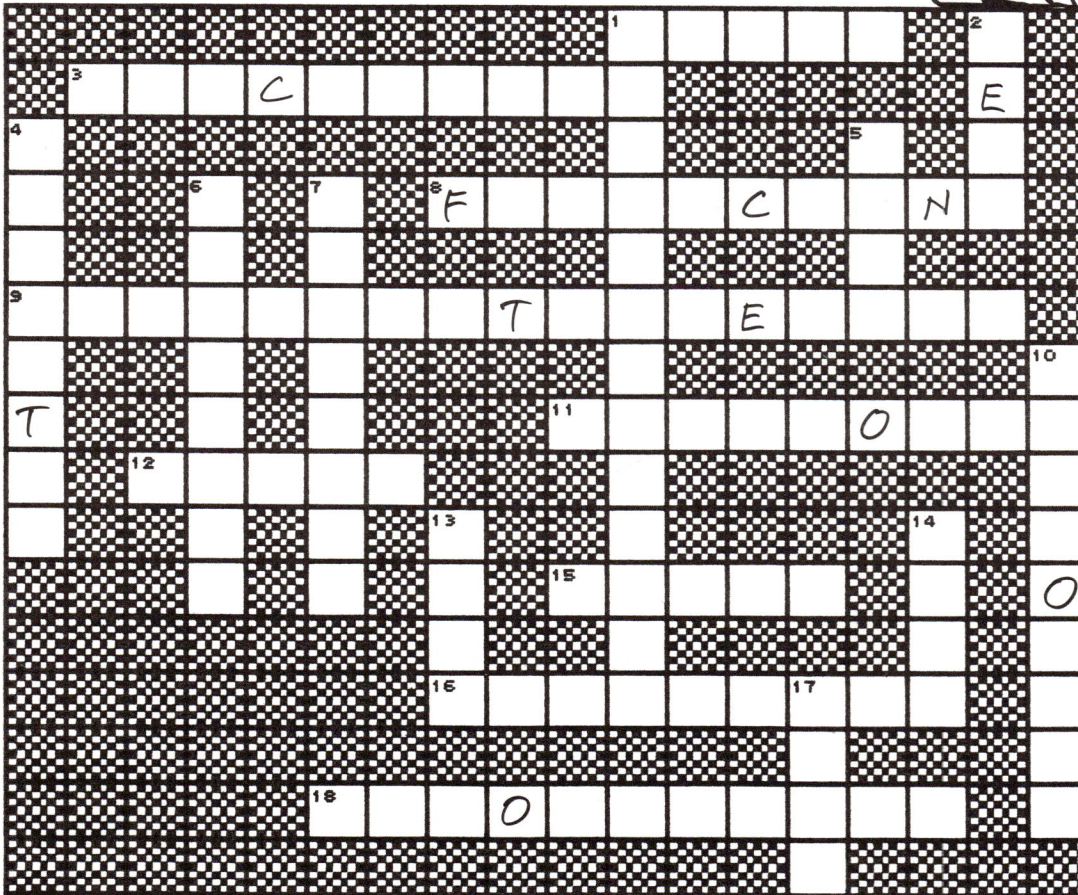

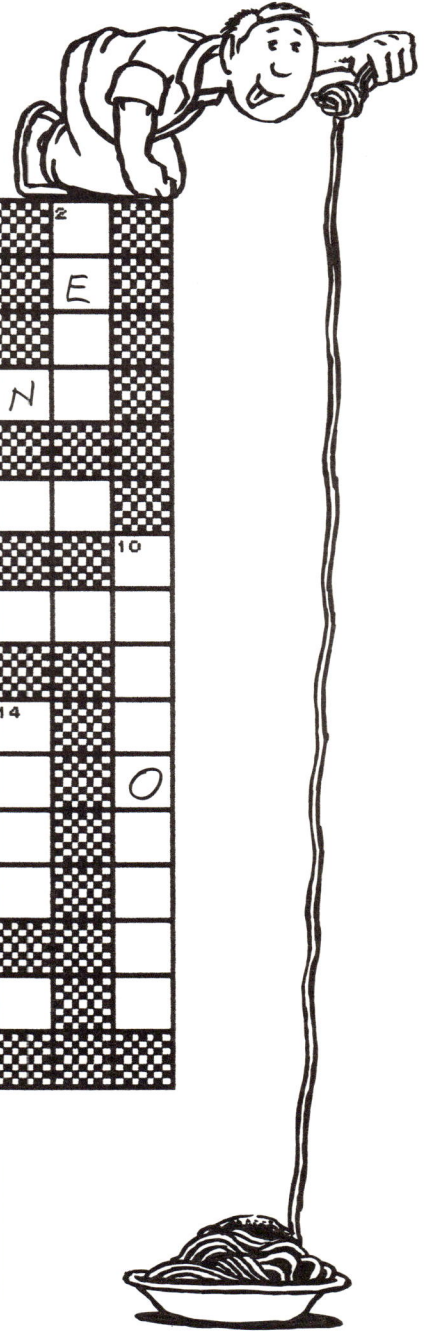

J. Da + the definite article.

There are many ways of translating **da** but its most common meaning is <u>from.</u>
e.g. **Vengo dall'aeroporto.** I'm coming from the airport.

In the same way that **a + il = al, da + il = dal.**
The two English words <u>from the</u> become just one word in Italian.

Complete this chart:

	il	l'	lo	la	i	gli	le
a+	al				ai		alle
da+							

SCRIVIAMO

K. Dal meaning <u>to the</u>.

> **Andare al:** to go to the place.
>
> **Andare dal:** to go to somebody's place.
>
> **Da** + *definite article* can also mean <u>to the</u>. We have already seen
> how **andare a** + *definite article* is used to say <u>you're going to a certain place</u>:
> e.g. **Vado all'ufficio postale.**
>   I'm going to the post office.
> If you want to say you're going to somebody's place,
> you use **andare da** + *definite article*:
> e.g. **Vado dal dottore.**
>   I'm going to the doctor's.

Fill in the gaps with the correct form of either <u>a</u> or <u>da</u>:

☑ Vado *alla* farmacia.

☑ Vado *dal* farmacista.

1. Marisa va _____ sarta, perchè vuole un nuovo vestito.

2. Perchè vai _____ ufficio postale?

3. Andiamo _____ stazione per incontrare gli zii.

4. Hanno sempre i capelli corti perchè vanno sempre _____ barbiere.

5. Andate _____ discoteca questo sabato?

6. Vado _____ dottore perchè sto male.

7. Perchè non vuoi andare _____ dentista?

8. Ho comprato i francobolli _____ tabaccaio.

L. Your friends know you study Italian and expect you to do all the talking when you go out together to an Italian restaurant. Show them you can handle the situation. Express in Italian: ✪✪✪

1. Excuse me, do you have a table for four?

_____

2. No, I'm sorry, we haven't booked.

_____

3. We've read the menu but we can't decide.

_____

4. Do you have to have a first course?

_____

5. No thanks, I don't like soup.

_____

6. Yes please, I like beans.

_____

7. Excuse me, what do you suggest?

_____

8. These fettucine are delicious!

_____

9. We're in a hurry, we have to catch a train.

_____

10. May we have the bill, please?

_____

11. Crikey! Three thousand lire for bread and cover charge!

_____

12. If they don't take Diners Club, we've had it.

_____

M. Imagine you are the waiter at the restaurant where
Mrs. Casati and the students ate. Read through the cartoon
strip and work out what they ate and how much it could cost.
Use the menu on page 108 as a guide.
Then fill out this bill: ⭐⭐

Extra vocabulary:

N. (numero)	number
importo	cost
IVA	Tax

TRATTORIA
I Tre Ladroni

DATA		N. Persone
10 LUGLIO		7

DITTA / SIG. CASATI

N.	Descrizione	IMPORTO
	COPERTO E PANE	
	VINO	
	ACQUA MINERALE E BIBITE	
	ANTIPASTI	
	PRIMI PIATTI	
	SECONDO DI CARNE	
	SECONDO DI PESCE	
	CONTORNI	
	FORMAGGIO	
	FRUTTA	
	DOLCE	
	PIZZE	
	CAFFE'	

TOTALE CORRISPETTIVO (IVA inclusa)		
Tavolo 5	IVA 10%	TOTALE

N. Parole crociate - fruit and vegetables. ⭐⭐

Orizzontali

2. Ottimi per i muscoli. (Braccio di Ferro)
4. Mi trovi nei campi in autunno
5. Plum
8. Cento grammi
9. Pears
11. Per fare il vino
13. Frutta tropicale
15. Apricot
16. Dieci etti
17. Insalata verde
18. Necessario per cucinare alla napoletana

Verticali

1. Nel Messico questi saltano in aria
3. Cibo preferito dai conigli
4. Ottima con panna o con gelato
6. È una pianta, sì, ma un uovo?!
7. Se mangi questa non hai bisogno del medico
9. Sono piccoli e verdi
10. Mangio questa frutta quando ho sete
12. Frutta coltivata in Sicilia
14. Necessario per fare il coleslaw

O. Below you will find six lists of ingredients which are used to make some of the Italian dishes found on page 108 of the textbook. Work out which dish you would make with each set of ingredients. Write the name of the dish and say for which course you would probably serve it: ★★

grattuggiato grated   **tritata** minced

1. **pasta, patate, piselli, carote, cipolla, fagioli:**

_____

_____

2. **carne, pane grattuggiato, uovo, olio, sale, pepe:**

_____

_____

3. **albicocche, ananas, angurie, ciliege, uva, melone:**

_____

_____

4. **riso, carne tritata, peperoni, sale, pepe, olio:**

_____

_____

5. **cetriolo, lattuga, verdure varie, aceto, olio:**

_____

_____

6. **sugo, pasta, prosciutto, piselli, uova:**

_____

_____

P. Il menù. ★★

You've just opened a trendy looking Italian restaurant. The chef you've hired has just handed you a list of all the things he can cook. Now you have to organise the list into a proper menu, including English explanations. (Some you'll know, some you'll work out, others you'll find out about).

osso buco
brodo con polpettine di carne
torta di mele alla panna
zuppa di vongole
funghi marinati
risotto alle verdure

cavolfiore alla napoletana
gelato al limone
fagioli al pomodoro
zuppa di cozze
insalata di calamari
spaghetti ad aglio e olio

pomodori ripieni
pollo alla Marsala
cannelloni
scaloppine alla panna
arance glassate
spirali e spinaci

ANTIPASTI

1._____

_____

2._____

_____

PRIMI
Minestre

1._____

_____

2._____

_____

3._____

_____

Pasta

1._____

_____

2._____

_____

3._____

_____

Riso

1._____

_____

SECONDI

1._____

_____

2._____

_____

3._____

_____

CONTORNI

1._____

_____

2._____

_____

3._____

_____

DOLCI

1._____

_____

2._____

_____

3._____

_____

Q. Use of the definite article. Express the following in Italian: ★ ★

1. Many tourists come to Australia from Japan.

_____

2. If you're going to Italy why don't you come to Sicily?

_____

3. Umbria is beautiful but I prefer Tuscany.

_____

4. They're coming from Holland next year.

_____

5. Students at this school don't study German.

_____

6. Tuscany is a large region in central Italy.

_____

7. Americans are very generous.

_____

8. The United States are in third place.

_____

R. Scrivere una lettera. How would you begin and end a letter to the following people?

☑ your brother	*Caro fratello,*	*Affettuosi saluti,*
☑ a lawyer	*Egregio avvocato,*	*Distinti saluti,*
1. your mother		
2. your teacher		
3. a woman you don't know		
4. a doctor		
5. your best friend		
6. a friend of the family		

S Un po' di tutto. ★ ★ ★
If you can express the following in Italian you can feel confident that you have mastered the material in Chapter 8. The letter(s) in brackets refers to a Parliamo exercise which you should find helpful.

1. Franca is coming but Marina can't come. (A,B)

_____

2. Gregorio says that the Dipierdomenico's are coming at six. (C)

_____

3. This pensione is too old. Can we go to the other one? (D)

_____

4. I know you don't want to go but you have to go. (E)

_____

5. Just a minute, Renzo, you can't go now. (F)

_____

6. They prefer to go from the pensione to the museum. (G,H)

_____

7. You haven't packed the cases and you have to write home. (I)

_____

8. Haven't I already closed the window? (J)

_____

9. Excuse me, sir. Listen, do you know where there's a plumber? (K, L)

_____

10. I like the salami but I'll have a kilo of mortadella. (M,N)

_____

T. Componimento: Saluti da Capri. ✪✪✪
   While your friends are toiling away back at school you're continuing your tour of Italy. Make them really envious by writing back a letter or postcard telling them about your trip to Capri. What did you see. what did you do, who did you meet, etc.?

_____

_____

_____

_____

_____

_____

_____

_____

_____

_____

_____

_____

U. Parole crociate - capitolo otto (revisione).

Orizzontali
4. Make yourselves comfortable!
8. Enjoy your meal! (2 words)
10. Fresh
13. Mixed
15. a + il
16. Un po' ... sale.
17. ... minerale
18. Unfortunately
20. How many of you are there? (3 words)
21. She, you (formal)
22. Con zucchero o ... zucchero?
24. Plate, dish

Verticali
1. Bread
2. I can't stand (3 words)
3. With
5. Diamoci del ...
6. Prendo i ravioli anch' ...
7. What would you like? (3 words)
9. Be', dunque, vediamo un po', ...
11. Cup
12. It doesn't matter (2 words)
13. But
14. Che ... squisito che viene dalla cucina.
19. i.e.
21. He
23. Andiamo al ristorante anche ...

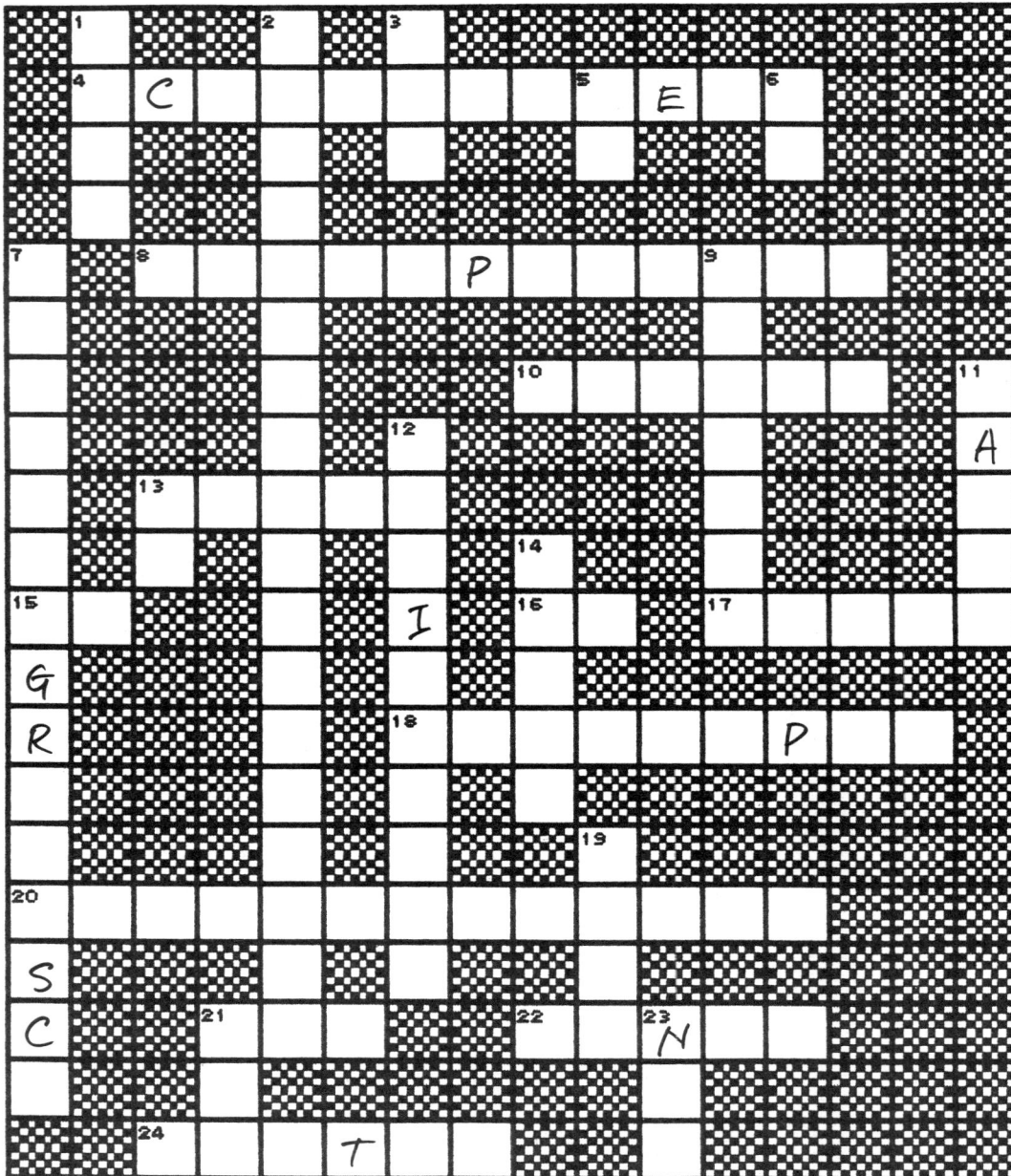

A. Capri. ★★
Answer the following questions which refer to the Cultural Unit, on pages 114-117 of the textbook:

1. Quanti anni ha Gina?_____

2. Dov'è Ercolano?_____

3. Che cosa deve fare Gina se vuole andare a Capri?_____
   _____

4. Quale autobus prendono Gina e Franco?_____
   _____

5. Come si va da Napoli a Capri?_____

6. Chi paga i biglietti per il traghetto?_____
   _____

7. Com'è il tempo oggi?_____

8. Che cosa vuole fare Gina ad Anacapri?_____
   _____

9. Come si va dalla Marina Grande ad Anacapri?_____
   _____

10. Come sono le vie di Anacapri?_____
    _____

B. Capri. ★
Write vero or falso after the following statements referring to the Cultural Unit, pages 114-117 of the textbook:

1. Gina non vuole mangiare. _____

2. Franco prende una bistecca. _____

3. Gina non vuole mangiare la cotoletta. _____

4. Dopo il conto Franco non ha molti soldi. _____

5. Franco vuole prenotare un viaggio di nozze. _____

6. Franco è contento di abitare a Napoli. _____

Suggested cultural background reading:
Regions of Italy, pages 54-57, Molise.

C. Il conto. A few weeks after their Capri outing Franco and Gina went to Amalfi. On this occasion they were much more careful about where they ate and how much they spent. Look carefully at this bill and answer the following questions in Italian. For some questions you may have to give your opinion.

☺ Hanno preso un secondo?

No, non hanno preso un secondo.

1. Che tipo di ristorante è?

2. Qual'è l'indirizzo?

3. Secondo te quanti primi piatti ha preso Franco?

4. Secondo te perchè non hanno preso un secondo?

5. Hanno mangiato zuppa di pesce? È possibile?

6. Hanno mangiato una pesca? È possibile?

7. Hanno preso una pizza Margherita?

8. Hanno bevuto un'aranciata? È possibile?

9. Hanno pagato molto secondo te?

RICEVUTA FISCALE - FATTURA (ricevuta fisc.) - Art. 1 e 2 D.M. 13-10-1979.

XAB N° 166813 /84

TRATTORIA - PIZZERIA
" S. GIUSEPPE "
Sede: Salita Ruggiero II, 4
Domicilio fiscale: Via Truglio, 18
☎ 872640 - 84011 A M A L F I (SA)
Cod. Fisc. MUO RSO 63L68 A251T
Partita IVA 01922030653

DATA	N.Persone
24.05.	2

DITTA / SIG. *FRANCO RANIERI*

N.	Descrizione	IMPORTO
2	COPERTO E PANE	2000
	VINO	
1	ACQUA MINERALE E BIBITE	1200
	ANTIPASTI	
4	PRIMI PIATTI	9000
	SECONDO DI CARNE	
	SECONDO DI PESCE	
	CONTORNI	
	FORMAGGIO	
2	FRUTTA	2600
	DOLCE	
	PIZZE	
	CAFFE'	

TOTALE CORRISPETTIVO (IVA Inclusa)	14800

Tavolo	IVA 10%	TOTALE
7		14800

Tip. U. De Rosa - Via N. Chiunzi, 71 - Maiori - Aut. Min. N. 367527 del 13-11-79

CAPITOLO NOVE

ALLA STAZIONE

ASCOLTIAMO

A. What are these people going to do? Write the appropriate number next to each description. The first one is done for you:

Going on a day trip.   (1.)

Having a shower.   ( )

Packing suitcases.   ( )

Going for a drive in the car.   ( )

Having breakfast.   ( )

Going for a ride on a bicycle.   ( )

Going on a picnic.   ( )

Going on a trip.   ( )

Washing dishes.   ( )

Going for a short walk.   ( )

B. What are these people ordering? Write down the English equivalent:

☑ *A lemonade with ice.*

1. _____

2. _____

3. _____

4. _____

5. _____

6. _____

7. _____

8. _____

9. _____

10. _____

SCRIVIAMO

A. Domande sul fumetto. ⭐

1. Perchè i ragazzi non sono contenti?

_____

2. È vero che la signora Casati non fa mai errori?

_____

3. Che cosa domanda Dario allo sportello?

_____

4. Da dove parte il prossimo treno per Catania?

_____

5. Dove sono i biglietti?

_____

6. Perchè non possono salire subito sul treno?

_____

7. Chi aspetta Angela in Sicilia?

_____

8. È vero che Adolfo non vuole aiutare?

_____

9. Come sta la zia Concetta?

_____

10. Che cosa ha Angela nella valigia?

_____

B. More on articulated prepositions.

Not all prepositions join with the definite article to make one word.
Here is a complete list of those that do.

Study this table:							
	il	lo	l'	la	i	le	gli
a	al	allo	all'	alla	ai	alle	agli
da	dal	dallo	dall'	dalla	dai	dalle	dagli
di	del	dello	dell'	della	dei	delle	degli
in	nel	nello	nell'	nella	nei	nelle	negli
su	sul	sullo	sull'	sulla	sui	sulle	sugli

e.g. **I ragazzi sono al ristorante.**
The kids are at the restaurant.

Questa lettera è dallo zio Rinaldo.
This letter is from uncle Rinaldo.

Sono nella tasca dell' altra giacca.
They're in the pocket of the other jacket.

La destinazione è sugli altri biglietti.
The destination is on the other tickets.

Note: Articulated forms of the preposition **con** (with) are not as common as those above, but you will occasionally come across **col, coll'** and **coi**.

e.g. **È arrivato col (con il) treno delle sette.**
He arrived on the seven o'clock train.

SCRIVIAMO

Place the underlined articulated preposition in front of the following words and then change the expression into the plural: ★

☺ (a) ristorante   *al ristorante*   *ai ristoranti*

1. (da) binario _____ _____

2. (in) cuore _____ _____

3. (di) infermiera _____ _____

4. (in) ospedale _____ _____

5. (di) scompartimento _____ _____

6. (su) giornale _____ _____

7. (su) altra _____ _____

8. (di) zaino _____ _____

We say that an article appeared <u>in</u> the paper. Italians find articles written <u>on</u> **(su)** their newspapers.

C. Complete the following sentences by writing the appropriate articulated preposition: ★★

1. Abbiamo ricevuto una lettera _____ zio di Giorgio.

2. La signora Casati non può ricordare il nome _____ pensione.

3. Voglio guardare le borsette _____ negozi di Roma.

4. Abbiamo letto la storia _____ bomba e _____ terroristi _____ giornali di ieri.

5. La valigia _____ signor Buzzati è _____ altro banco.

6. Non ricordo più il numero _____ scompartimento.

7. Ho ricevuto questa cartolina _____ amici che abitano a Wagga Wagga.

8. Vorrei fare l'astronauta perchè voglio camminare _____ luna.

9. Posso mettere un po' di cioccolato _____ latte?

10. Adesso bisogna mettere il sugo _____ spaghetti e _____ fettucine. Sono _____ dente!

D. Find out how articulated prepositions were used by characters in the cartoon script in expressing the following: ★★

1. That evening at 9:45 p.m.

_____

2. The kids arrive at the station but the train's not there.

_____

3. Just a minute, I'll ask at the ticket window.

_____

4. There's a train that leaves for Catania from platform nineteen.

_____

5. They're in the pocket of the jacket.

_____

6. No, they're in the other pocket.

_____

7. Why don't you put us with the cases in the luggage compartment?

_____

8. If you like I'll put you on the roof or I'll tie you to the wheels.

_____

9. Tomorrow she has to come out of hospital with the nurse.

_____

10. O.K., quick, get on the train!

_____

E. Negative expressions.

Non dice niente.	He's saying nothing. (He's not saying anything).
Non parla mai.	He never speaks.
Non ho visto nessuno.	I saw nobody. (I didn't see anyone).

In English it is incorrect to use a *double negative*.
Use the following sentence to help you understand why this is so:
"He's not saying nothing."
In Italian double negative expressions are used with **niente** (nothing),
nessuno (no-one) and **mai** (never) and the meaning of the sentence remains negative.

Non dice
mai niente!

What do the following sentences mean?

1. Ha parlato molto ma non ha detto niente.

_____

2. Abbiamo cercato tutta la mattina ma non abbiamo trovato niente.

_____

3. Non hanno mai letto questa lettera.

_____

4. Non ho mai visto tua zia.

_____

5. Non conosco nessuno in questa classe.

_____

6. Non abbiamo incontrato nessuno qui.

_____

F. These negative expressions may also be used in the following ways:

Che cosa hai detto?	What did you say?
Niente.	Nothing.
Hai mai visto mia zia?	Have you ever seen my aunt?
Mai.	Never.
Chi hai incontrato?	Who did you meet?
Nessuno.	No-one
Chi vuole aiutare?	Who wants to help?
Nessuno.	Nobody.

Translate into Italian: ★★★

1. I'm listening but I hear nothing.

2. I'm sure that they have done nothing.

3. I have nothing but I'm happy.

4. He never listens when we speak.

5. They have never cleaned the spark plugs.

6. He never tells the truth. Never!

7. I looked for the children but I didn't find anyone.

8. He didn't speak with anybody.

9. Nobody listens to Giorgio.

10. What did we do? Nothing! Who did we meet? No-one!

G. Fare expressions. ★
Use the list of fare expressions on page 132 of the textbook to help you do the following. Express in English:

1. Sei così antipatica quando fai il muso.

2. Vuoi fare una passeggiata questo pomeriggio?

3. Perchè non facciamo un giro in bicicletta?

4. Gregorio non è più meccanico. Adesso fa l'idraulico.

5. Perchè devi sempre fare la stupida?

6. Hai perso i biglietti? Be', non fa niente.

H. Dov'è Giorgio?

You've seen this little episode before. Fill in the bubbles in your own words, without looking at ... and certainly without copying from the textbook. Remember what happened? Giorgio orders some food including a piece of pizza. Since the pizza is sold by the **etto** he asks for **10 etti,** not knowing that that makes 1 kilo. Throughout, he insists that he's not very hungry, not a glutton and he doesn't eat much.

1. Giorgio: _____

2. Signorina: _____

3. Giorgio: _____

_____

_____

_____

4. Signorina: _____

5. Giorgio: _____

6. Signorina: _____

7. Giorgio: _____

_____

_____

I. Express in Italian: ★★★

1. I would like to be part of this team. _____

_____

2. Why are you pretending to be intelligent? _____

_____

3. We're going on a trip in October._____

4. They're having a chat._____

5. I never have breakfast._____

6. The weather's lovely today._____

J. Parole nuove. ⭐

1. **Which doesn't belong?**

fare una passeggiata   fare una doccia   fare una gita   fare un giro in auto   _____

2. **Which wouldn't you drink?**

l'aranciata   il chinotto   l'arancino   il succo di frutta   _____

3. **Which wouldn't you put in your tea?**

il latte   lo zucchero   il miele   la salsa   _____

4. **Which won't help much when you're ravenous?**

il ghiaccio   il tramezzino   il panino imbottito   le paste   _____

5. **Which expression is more like something the customer would say?**

mi dica   prego   mi dia   desidera   _____

6. **Which will not make the shopkeeper happy?**

ne prendo un chilo   non voglio niente   ne voglio un etto   mi dia due etti   _____

K. Adverbs.

-ly = -mente			
adjective		*adverb*	
alto	high	**altamente**	highly
triste	sad	**tristemente**	sadly
debole	weak	**debolmente**	weakly
regolare	regular	**regolarmente**	regularly
buono	good	**bene**	well
cattivo	bad	**male**	badly

e.g. **Mi ha parlato severamente.**
He spoke harshly to me.

Si veste sempre così elegantemente.
She always dresses so elegantly.

Teresa ha potuto fare tutto facilmente.
Teresa was able to do everything easily.

Parla bene ma scrive molto male.
He speaks well but writes very badly.

Write down the meaning of the following sentences: ⭐

1. Non potete salire: è assolutamente vietato.

_____

2. La vecchia infermiera ha parlato gentilmente.

_____

3. Gli svedesi hanno giocato fortemente.

_____

Which are the adverbs in the sentences above?

_____

In sentences 2 and 3, what is the function of the adverbs?

_____

L. Adverbs.

modesto → modestamente
alto → altamente
triste → tristemente

In English you form this type of adverb by adding -ly to the adjective. How do you do it in Italian?

_____

_____

debole → debolmente
regolare → regolarmente

What is the rule for adjectives ending in **-re** and **-le**?

_____

_____

Form adverbs from the following adjectives: ★

1. severo	_____	7. facile	_____
2. freddo	_____	8. pericoloso	_____
3. sciocco	_____	9. preciso	_____
4. tranquillo	_____	10. terribile	_____
5. squisito	_____	11. stupido	_____
6. felice	_____	12. leggero	_____

Take special note of these: **buono** (good) → **bene** (well)
cattivo (bad) → **male** (badly)

M. Translate into Italian: ★★

1. He dresses very elegantly.

_____

2. I explained the problem clearly.

_____

3. They spoke freely to the waiter.

_____

4. The kids undress quickly.

_____

5. He doesn't speak French very well.

_____

6. He has done everything badly.

_____

N. Fare expressions. ★★
Under each drawing write in Italian what is being done. Make the verbs agree with the subjects given:

☺ Io *faccio i piatti.*

1. Noi _____

2. Tu _____

_____

3. Lui _____

O. Che cosa piace a Laura? ★★★
In the spaces below, fill in the answers to the following questions.
When you have done this you will find in the vertical column,
what Laura likes doing most of all:

1. A good tea in summer
2. Fanta is one type
3. Non è contento
4. An Italian style sandwich
5. Some people prefer it with minerals
6. Juice
7. A Sicilian rice snack
8. It goes well with tea and coffee
9. A snack
10. The ticket window
11. An Italian cola drink.
12. To remember
13. He helps with the luggage
14. Where you catch the train
15. Normalmente è imbottito
16. Too much is not good for you
17. To happen
18. Added to drinks on hot days
19. A type of chesse
20. Have some only if you're not sweet enough
21. Where you put your money
22. Freshly squeezed juice

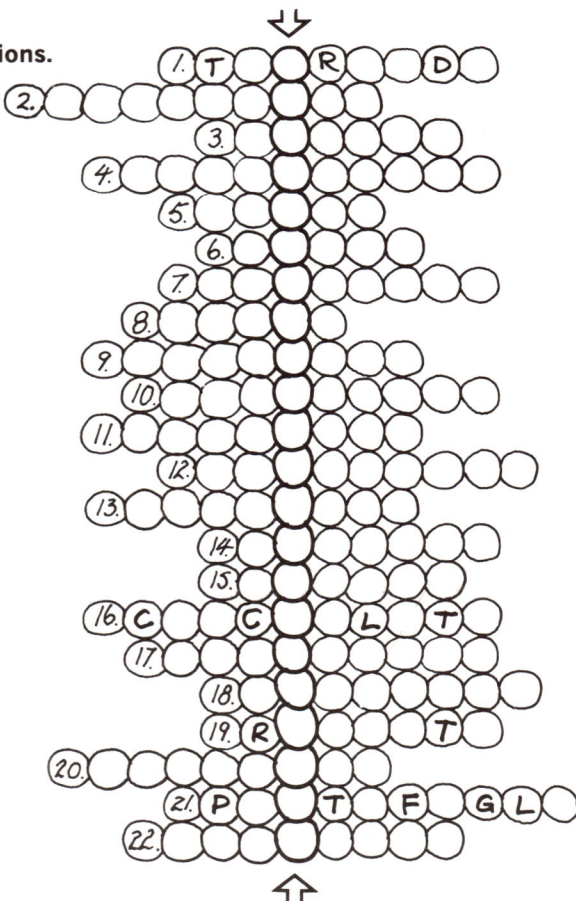

P. Conjunctive personal pronouns. Mi, ti, ci, vi.

> **mi** me, to me
> e.g. **Mi capisce?** Do you understand me? (**Lei** form)
> **Mi parli?** Will you speak to me? (**tu** form)
> **ti** you (sing.), to you
> e.g. **Questo facchino non ti aiuta.** This porter is not helping you.
> **Ti do il libro.** I'll give the book to you.
> **ci** us, to us
> e.g. **Perchè non ci mette con le valige?** Why don't you put us with the cases?
> **Ci parla spesso.** He often speaks to us.
> **vi** you (pl.), to you
> e.g. **Se volete vi metto sul tetto.** If you wish I'll put you on the roof.
> **Vi danno la nuova macchina?** Will they give the new car to you?

Find out how <u>mi, ti, ci</u> or <u>vi</u> were used by characters in the cartoon script in expressing the following: ★★

1. Aunt Concetta has to meet me tomorrow morning._____

_____

2. This porter is not listening to you, he doesn't believe you._____

_____

3. Thanks, Adolfo, I'll never forget you!_____

4. But sir, can't you help us?_____

5. She's waiting for us at six in the morning._____

6. I'll tie you to the wheels._____

7. Will I help you with the suitcases?_____

Q. How would you say...? ★★★

1. They have to call me tomorrow morning._____

_____

2. Quick, Gina, we're waiting for you. (sing.)_____

_____

3. I'm sorry, but I never listen to you. (sing.)_____

_____

4. Can't you meet us at the station?_____

_____

5. She's calling us after lunch._____

6. I'll put you (pl.) on the roof._____

7. Will I meet you on platform 6?_____

R. Un po' di tutto.
If you can express the following sentences in Italian then you can feel confident that you have mastered the material in Chapter 9. The letter in brackets refers to a Parliamo exercise which you may find helpful.

1. I have never told a lie. (A)_____

2. The carabinieri didn't find out anything. (B)_____

_____

3. I'll wait for you in front of the supermarket. (D)_____

_____

4. They're meeting us at ten o'clock. (E)_____

_____

5. I never come because they never call me. (F)_____

_____

6. We can't go because no-one has booked the tickets. (G)_____

_____

7. They are the girls' suitcases. (H)_____

8. The soup, sir? Here it is now! (I)_____

9. The keys are in the handbag on the table. (J)_____

_____

10. They haven't asked anyone. (K)_____

11. So, you're working as a hairdresser now! (L)_____

_____

12. Do you want to go for a bit of a walk? (M)_____

_____

13. He did everything calmly. (N)_____

S. Componimento
Write a typical dialogue that would take place in a cafe, a generi alimentari, or at the ticket office of the train station. Your dialogue should include:

inquiring about something
asking about price, quality, type
completing a transaction.

Dove sei?_____   **Con chi parli?**_____

_____   _____

_____   _____

_____   _____

_____   _____

_____   _____

_____   _____

_____   _____

_____   _____

T. Componimento.

A friend of yours is planning to go to Italy soon. Since you're the local expert you've been asked to write down some handy phrases for use in practical situations. Make up a list of phrases explaining where you would use them and what they mean:

☑ **Al generi alimentari.** At the grocer's.

   Quanto costa il formaggio al chilo? How much does the cheese cost per kilo?

1._____

_____

2._____

_____

3._____

_____

Al bar._____

_____

1._____

_____

2._____

_____

3._____

_____

Alla stazione._____

1._____

_____

2._____

_____

3._____

_____

A. I treni Italiani.
Write vero or falso after the following statements referring to the Cultural Unit, I treni Italiani on pages 128-129 of the textbook:

1. I turisti che prendono i treni italiani viaggiano sicuramente e comodamente. _____

2. Molti viaggiatori prendono una cuccetta e così risparmiano il costo di un albergo o di una pensione. _____

3. Ci sono sempre molti posti liberi nei treni italiani. _____

4. C'è un treno che parte per la Sicilia da Roma dopo le undici di sera. _____

5. Non si può viaggiare in seconda classe con il Rapido. _____

6. Il Rapido si ferma a tutte le stazioni. _____

B. Tirrenia is a privately owned ferry service. It offers a similar service to that of the FS (Ferrovie dello Stato), the state owned company. Tirrenia operates in 14 ports, including two outside Italy. Label these ports on the map:

Napoli	Malta
Palermo	Trapani
Tunisi	Civitavecchia
Cagliari	Genova
Reggio Calabria	Porto Torres
Catania	Arbatax
Siracusa	Olbia

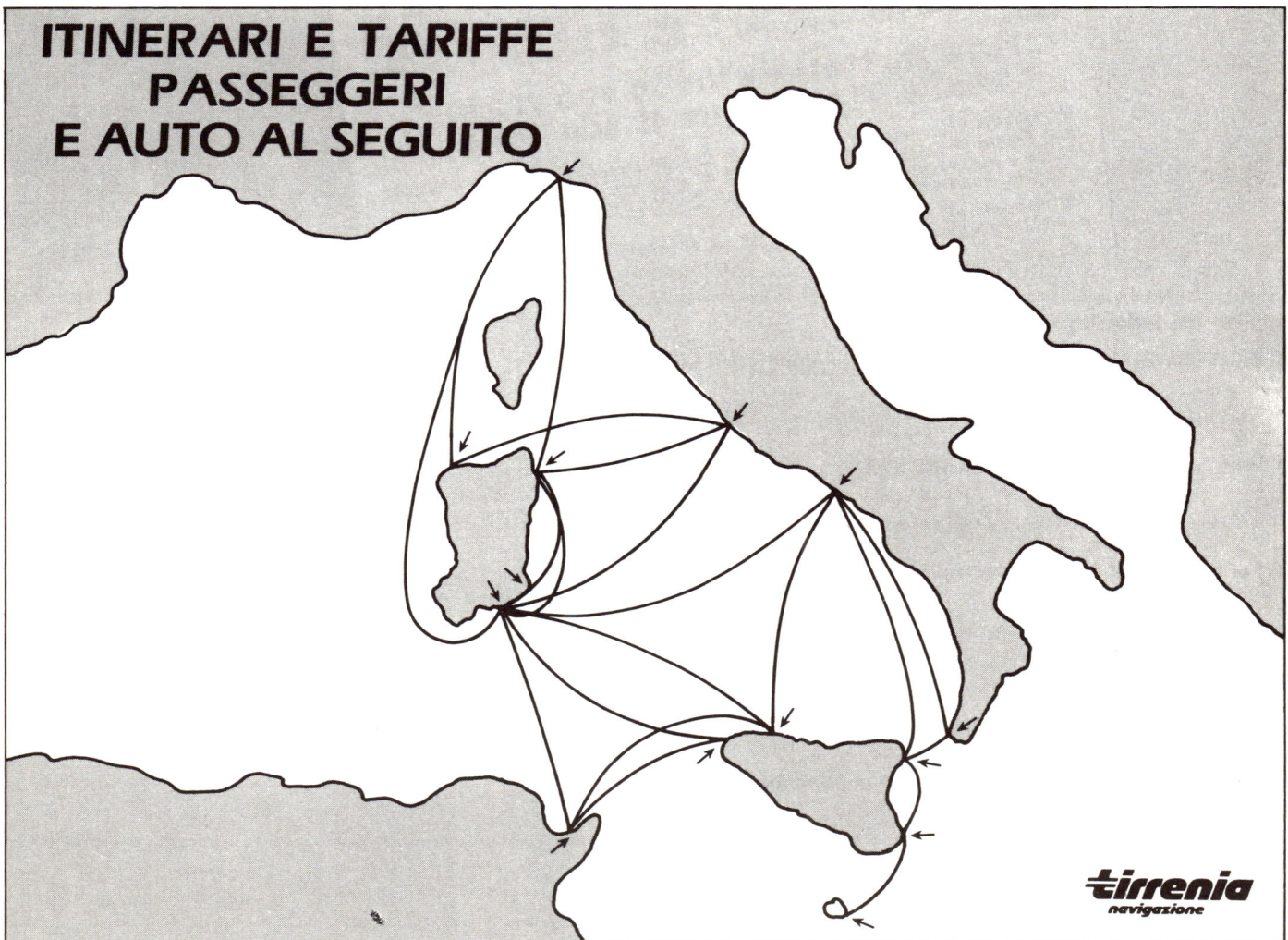

ITINERARI E TARIFFE PASSEGGERI E AUTO AL SEGUITO

tirrenia
navigazione

C. Biglietto chilometrico.
Without looking up every word in the dictionary, try to understand this notice about train travel in Italy.

INTER-RAIL
se hai meno di 26 anni ti fa
viaggiare per un mese in 20 paesi.

**uno sconto
per tutti
su 3.000 km.**

**GIOVANI
sotto i 26**

visitate l'EUROPA
in TRENO

con il biglietto

visitate l'EUROPA
in TRENO
CON IL BIGLIETTO

B.I.G.

biglietto chilometrico
viaggi per 3000 chilometri
con riduzione del **20%**

Il biglietto chilometrico è particolarmente utile e conveniente per le persone che, volendo viaggiare per qualsiasi motivo, singolarmente o in piccoli gruppi, non possono fruire di altre forme di riduzione, e per le aziende che abbiano necessità di far viaggiare il proprio personale singolarmente o contemporaneamente.

PREZZO DEL BIGLIETTO: **1ª classe lire 50.600** **2ª classe lire 28.600** VALIDITÀ: UN MESE

Il biglietto chilometrico, rilasciato per una percorrenza di 3000 chilometri, può essere utilizzato a più riprese, fino ad un massimo di 20 viaggi; è nominativo e può essere intestato fino ad un massimo di 5 persone che possono viaggiare insieme o separatamente.
La riduzione del 50% per i ragazzi da 4 a 14 anni è assicurata conteggiando a metà i chilometri di viaggio.

Answer the following questions in English:

1. What name might we give the biglietto chilometrico in English?

2. Who is eligible for a 1/2 price discount?

3. For how long is such a ticket valid?

4. How far can you travel?

5. How many people can travel together or separately on the same ticket?

6. What is the maximum number of stops you can make?

D. Train timetable.

1. Look carefully at this timetable then write vero or falso next to the following statements:

SIRACUSA - CATANIA / PALERMO } MESSINA - ROMA   Segue 6

	1 e 2	1 e 2	1 e 2	1 e 2	1 e 2	1 e 2	1 e 2	1 e 2	1 e 2	1 e 2
SIRACUSA ....p.	...	...	16 46	17 15	...	19 34	19 34	21 17	...	...
CATANIA ....p.	...	17 35	18 17	19 02	...	21 18	21 18	23 02	...	...
TAORMINA G. ..p.	...	18 21	19 04	20 04	...	22 14	22 14	23 58	...	...
MESSINA C. ...a.	...	18 57	19 40	20 45	...	23 05	23 05	0 38	...	...
PALERMO ....p.	...	...	...	...	17 47	19 30	19 30	21 10	...	22 45
MESSINA C. ...a.	...	...	...	...	21 34	23 12	23 12	0 38	...	4 30
MESSINA M. ..p.	...	19 35	20 25	21 25	22 15	23 55	0 45	1 40	...	7 20
REGGIO CAL. ..p.	20 18	20 32	20 58	22 02	22 55	0 35	1 12	2 18	7 05	7 48
VILLA S. GIOV. p.	20 54	21 15	21 45	22 55	23 55	1 15	2 05	3 00	7 28	8 34
LAMEZIA T. C. ..p.	23 13	22 37	23 04	0 18	1 05	2 30	3 26	4 19	8 54	10 47
PAOLA ......p.	0 11	23 14	23 39	0 57	1 44	3 05	4 05	5 01	9 30	11 34
SALERNO ....p.	2 56	1 49	2 14	3 45	4 37	5 29	7 03	8 31	12 16	15 29
NAPOLI C. ....p.	4 00	2 51	◊ 3 18	◊ 4 56	5 50	6 29	8 16	9 47	13 12	16 48
ROMA TERM. ..a.	6 45	: 5 13	: 5 28	7 36	8 28	8 36	10 40	12 40	15 18	19 47

■ 🚃 1ª cl. Reggio C.C.-Roma; ↦ 2ª cl. Palermo-Roma. 🚃 e ↦ 1ª e 2ª cl. Reggio C.C.-Roma.
* ↦ di 1ª e 2ª cl. Reggio C.C.-Roma e ↦ 2ª cl. Catania-Roma. 🚃 Reggio C.C.-Roma. 🚃 Agrigento-Caltanissetta-Catania-Roma.
: 🚃 Palermo e Reggio C.C.-Roma.
● ↦ 1ª e 2ª cl. Catania-Milano; 🚃 Reggio C.C.-Milano.

® 🚃 Reggio C.C.-Milano; 🚃 1ª cl. e ↦ di 1ª e 2ª cl.
◆ 🚃 Siracusa e Catania-Roma; 🚃 Palermo-Reggio C.C.-Roma; ↦ 2ª cl. Catania-Roma; ↦ 1ª e 2ª cl. Siracusa-Roma; ↦ 1ª e 2ª cl. Palermo-Roma; 🚃 1ª cl. Siracusa, Catania, Palermo e Messina-Roma.
◊ Napoli Campi Flegrei.   : Roma Tiburtina.

a) C'è un treno da Catania a Salerno che parte alle 5:35 del pomeriggio. _____

b) Il treno che parte da Siracusa alle 16:46 arriva a Paola dopo mezzanotte. _____

c) Non c'è un treno con cucette da Palermo a Napoli. _____

d) Ci vogliono più di sei ore da Messina a Napoli in treno. _____

2. Now answer these questions in Italian:

a) A che ora arriva a Salerno il treno delle 17:35 da Catania?

_____

b) Sono a Taormina. C'è un treno che arriva a Napoli verso le 8:00? Se c'è, a che ora parte?

_____

c) A che ora parte l'ultimo treno da Siracusa?

_____

d) A che ora parte da Messina il primo treno dopo mezzanotte? Quando arriva a Napoli?

_____

Suggested cultural background reading: Regions of Italy, pages 62-70, Valle d'Aosta and Friuli-Venezia Giulia.

CAPITOLO DIECI

SUL TRENO

Suggested cultural background reading: Regions of Italy, pages 24-27, Calabria.

ASCOLTIAMO

A. Guess where these people are: in a bank, or at the supermarket, or perhaps at the swimming pool. Write your answer in English:

☺ At the post office.

1. _____

2. _____

3. _____

4. _____

5. _____

6. _____

7. _____

8. _____

9. _____

10. _____

B. What does this lady have to do before she is ready? Write the appropriate number next to each description:

☺ She has to wake up.   (   )

She has to shave her legs.   (   )

She has to lie down.   (   )

She has to comb herself.   (   )

She has to dress herself.   (   )

She has to get angry.   (   )

She has to wash herself.   (   )

A. Domande sul fumetto:

1. Com'è la signora Casati, è contenta?_____

2. Perchè i ragazzi si devono coricare presto?_____

_____

3. A che ora si devono alzare?_____

4. Che cosa fanno i ragazzi, prima di coricarsi?_____

_____

5. Quanto tempo ci vuole prima che si addormenta la signora Casati?_____

_____

6. Che cosa vogliono fare i ragazzi?_____

_____

7. Come sanno se la signora Casati dorme?_____

_____

8. Perchè Giorgio dice a Kevin di stare tranquillo?_____

_____

9. Secondo te, le ragazze capiscono Giorgio?_____

_____

10. Gli amici delle ragazze hanno paura di Giorgio?_____

B. Parole nuove. ★★

1. Someone has just asked to use your telephone. Which response would leave the other person most startled?

   faccia pure s'accomodi tanti auguri prego _____

2. You've just asked someone where to get off the bus for the Pantheon in Rome.
   Which response would indicate that the other person has misunderstood?

   alla prossima fermata al capolinea alle nove dopo Piazza Venezia _____

3. Which are out of place?

   cartoline tortellini francobolli pacchi _____

4. "Può firmare, per favore?" Which of these would that question not refer to?

   il modulo la patente gli assegni gli spiccioli _____

5. Which won't you have to pay?

   la tariffa l'uscita il conto il prezzo _____

6. Which are you most likely to find in a cabina telefonica?

   un telefono un gettone l'elenco telefonico un'altra persona _____

SCRIVIAMO

C. Reflexive verbs.

		svegli**arsi**	to wake (oneself) up
io	**mi**	svegli**o**	I wake up
tu	**ti**	svegl**i**	you wake up
lui, lei	**si**	svegli**a**	he, she wakes up
noi	**ci**	sveglia**mo**	we wake up
voi	**vi**	svegli**ate**	you wake up
loro	**si**	svegli**ano**	they wake up

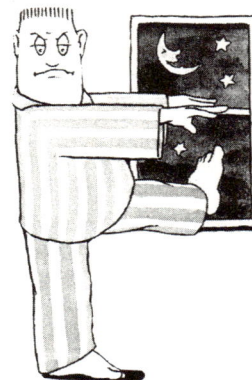

Study these two sentences:

La signora Casati sveglia i ragazzi alle sei e mezzo.

La signora Casati si sveglia alle sei e mezzo.

In which of these sentences is the verb **svegliare** used *reflexively?*_____

_____

What does the word *reflexively* mean in this context?_____

_____

Of course, in English the *-self* word, which makes the verb obviously reflexive, is very often omitted.
With reflexive verbs in Italian the reflexive pronoun (**mi, ti, si,** etc.) is always used.
Not all Italian reflexive verbs are as obviously reflexive as svegliarsi.
e.g. **sbagliarsi:** to make a mistake.

Here is a list of reflexive verbs which occur in this chapter:

addo**ment**arsi to fall asleep
alz**arsi** to get up
cori**carsi** to lie down
divert**irsi** to enjoy yourself/oneself
lav**arsi** to wash (oneself)
pettin**arsi** to comb one's hair
rad**ersi** to shave
sbagli**arsi** to make a mistake
spogli**arsi** to undress
svegli**arsi** to wake up

Write an English equivalent for the following: ⭐

1. Si addormenta sotto la tavola._____

2. Vi divertite qui a Roma?

_____

3. Perchè non ti corichi sopra il banco?

_____

4. I ragazzi si spogliano velocemente._____

5 Io mi sveglio alle sette ma mi alzo alle otto.

_____

6. Lei si sbaglia, signora._____

7. Ci sbagliamo spesso!_____

8. Dove posso pettinarmi?_____

D. Complete the following sentences by writing the appropriate <u>present tense</u> form of the infinitive in brackets: ★★

1. In prima classe Giorgio e Dario _____ (divertirsi) un mondo.

2. Ma io non _____ (addormentarsi) mai a quest'ora.

3. Presto, ragazzi, sono le sei e mezzo. Perchè non _____ (svegliarsi)?

4. I giornalisti _____ (sbagliarsi) spesso.

5. Luciano ed io _____ (vestirsi) alla pensione.

6. Giorgio, tu _____ (radersi) ogni giorno?

7. Signorina, se Lei è ammalata perchè non _____ (coricarsi) qui?

8. Faye _____ (vestirsi) così elegantemente.

E. Giorgio allowed us to take some shots of him going about his daily routine. ★★
You have to provide the captions for the pictures. Use reflexive verbs for each one.

Mattina:

☑ _Giorgio si sveglia._   1. _____   2. _____

3. _____   4. _____   5. _____

Sera:

6. _____   7. _____   8. _____

9. _____   10. _____   11. _____

F. | **Some common reflexive verbs refer to the way people react to things:**

annoi**arsi**   to get bored
arrabbi**arsi**   to get angry
meravig i**arsi**   to be surprised
vergogn**arsi**   to be ashamed, embarrassed
preoccup**arsi** to get worried

La signora Casati
si arrabbia facilmente.

Explain how you react in the following situations: ★★
Come reagisci quando...?

1. La mamma ti compra un regalo e non è il tuo compleanno.

_____

2. La mamma trova che non hai detto la verità.

_____

3. La mamma dice come sei bravo/a quando parla con le amiche.

_____

4. La mamma ti punisce e non è colpa tua.

_____

5. La mamma dice, "Devi coricarti adesso", durante il tuo programma preferito.

_____

6. Devi fare i piatti e poi lavorare in giardino.

_____

G. Reflexive infinitives. ★★
Study the way reflexive infinitives **are used in these sentences. See if you can work out what they mean in English:**

1. Bisogna alzarsi presto domani.

_____

2. Dovete addormentarvi perchè vi dovete svegliare presto.

_____

3. Devo radermi più tardi.

_____

4. Non ti puoi radere adesso?

_____

5. Non si diverte perchè non sa divertirsi.

_____

6. Non puoi alzarti a quest'ora.

_____

H. You have to be careful not to lose the reflexive pronoun (<u>mi, ti, ci, vi, si</u>) when you use the infinitive of a reflexive verb. The pronoun may be either tacked on to the end of the infinitive or placed in front of a verb (e.g. potere, dovere, volere, sapere) that is used with an infinitive.   ★★★

Express in Italian:

☑ You're tired and you can't fall asleep.

Sei stanco e non puoi addormentarti.

1. You're fifteen and you don't know how to dress (yourself)!

_____

2. If you (pl.) want to get up early you have to go to sleep now.

_____

3. I have to do my hair, I can't go out like this.

_____

4. Is it really necessary to get undressed?

_____

I. The following words relate to either the bank, the post office, the bus stop or the telephone booth. Write them under the appropriate headings:

la buca, salire, la cabina, il gettone, il conto, la tariffa, il modulo, il pacco, il capolinea, il francobollo, l'assegno, via aerea, il prefisso, l'elenco, la cassa.

La fermata dell'autobus	La banca	L'ufficio postale	Il telefono pubblico

J. Complete the following sentences by writing the appropriate <u>present tense</u> of the verb in brackets. The line at the end of the sentence is for you to write the same verb in the <u>perfect tense</u>(revision).

1. I ragazzi _____ (investigare) gli scompartimenti in prima classe._____

2. La signora Casati _____ (dormire) bene durante il viaggio._____

3. Ma signore, perchè non _____ (capire) il problema di Angela?_____

4. Sì, sono sicurissimo, i ragazzi _____ (prendere) il treno._____

5. Io _____ (fare) i biglietti prima delle sette._____

6. Kevin _____ (dovere) spiegare tutto alla signora Casati._____

7. Dario, perchè _____ (dire) una stupida bugia?_____

8. Noi _____ (avere) molti problemi._____

Now, make sure you know the meaning of each of the above sentences.

K. Revision. You're on work experience in an Italian kindergarten (l'asilo infantile) and you're doing a unit on <u>La Posta.</u> Here is your explanation of what happens when you write a letter. Fill in the missing words. (They're all articulated prepositions.)

Scrivo la lettera _____ carta, poi metto la carta _____ busta. Scrivo l'indirizzo _____ amico

_____ busta. Compro un francobollo _____ tabaccaio e metto il francobollo _____ busta.

Poi vado _____ Ufficio Postale e metto la busta _____ buca.

Poi viene il postino che prende la busta _____ buca.

Il postino mette la busta _____ sacco con le altre buste. Porta il sacco _____ casa _____ amico.

L'amico gioca davanti _____ casa e così prende la lettera _____ mani _____ postino.

Interessante, no?!!

L. Revision. Write the following sentences in the plural:

1. La ragazza è ammalata.

_____

2. Questo binario è troppo vecchio e pericoloso.

_____

3. Lo scompartimento è veramente occupato.

_____

4. La tasca[1] della giacca[1] è piena di medicina.

_____

5. L'uomo[2] è svedese.

_____

6. L'ospedale in questa città è antico.

_____

Remember:
1. How are you going to keep the hard "k" sound in the plural?
2. An irregular plural: **uomini.**

M. Irregular verbs. Complete the following table:

	venire	bere	fare	sapere	salire	uscire
io	vengo					
tu		bevi				
lui, lei			fa			
noi				sappiamo		
voi					salite	
loro						escono

N. Polite imperatives with <u>pure</u>!

Faccia pure!	Go right ahead (and do it)!
Vada pure!	Go right ahead (and leave, go, etc.)!
S'accomodi pure!	Do take a seat! Make yourself comfortable
S'accomodi pure alla cassa!	Please go to the teller's counter.

Write one of the above commands next to the appropriate question:

☺ Posso andare? **Prego,** _vada pure._ _____!

1. È libero questo posto? **Prego,** _____!

2. Posso partire? **Prego,** _____!

3. I soldi sono pronti? **Prego,** _____!

4. Posso usare il telefono? **Prego,** _____!

5. Posso uscire? **Prego,** _____!

6. Permesso? **Prego,** _____!

7. Mi posso sedere? **Prego,** _____!

8. Posso prestare la penna? **Prego,** _____!

9. Posso entrare? **Prego,** _____!

10. Posso usare il bagno? **Prego,** _____!

O. Complete the following sentences by writing the appropriate form of the verb. The infinitive is in brackets:

1. Presto ragazzi, _____ (salire)! L'autobus è in partenza.

2. In quest'autobus si _____ (salire) davanti e si _____ (uscire) dietro.

3. Alla prossima fermata _____ (salire) tutti gli alunni dell'Istituto Tecnico.

4. Caterina, è vero che _____ (uscire) con Carlo sabato sera?

5. Giorgio, Dario e Kevin _____ (fare) brutta figura.

6. Se _____ (bere) caffè non posso dormire.

7. Dario non _____ (sapere) parlare alle ragazze.

8. Stasera io e Claudio _____ (uscire) insieme, ma _____ (venire) anche la mamma.

P. Sapere, conoscere (revision).
Insert the correct form of <u>sapere</u> or <u>conoscere</u> in the appropriate spaces. Remember, <u>sapere</u> means <u>to know how to do something,</u> while <u>conoscere</u> means <u>to be acquainted with</u>:

☺ Giorgio _____ Sa _____ parlare con le ragazze?

1. I ragazzi _____ guidare il motorino.

2. Scusi signore, _____ dov'è l'ufficio postale?

3. Non _____ tutti i monumenti ma abbiamo visitato L'Altare della Patria

CONTINUA

4. Voi _____ solo l'inglese, ma noi _____ anche l'italiano.

5. Clelia _____ suonare il pianoforte.

6. Chi? Clelia? Non la _____

7. Che ridicolo, hai gli sci e non _____ sciare.

Q. Come si chiama la ragazza di Dario?
Even though he might seem shy, Dario has a girlfriend.
Find out her name by completing the puzzle below:

1. Non voglio salire voglio …
2. Mi dispiace, non ho soldi, ho solo un …
3. Bisogna sapere questo per telefonare.
4. Lavora in banca.
5. Faye non ha scritto una lettera, ma ha mandato una …
6. La lettera non viaggia senza questi.
7. Una breve ma veloce comunicazione.
8. In banca bisogna riempire un … prima di depositare i soldi.
9. Non è l'uscita.

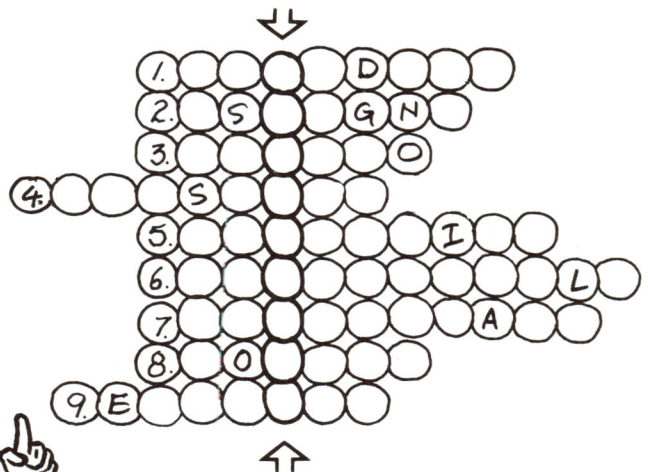

R. Un po' di tutto.
If you can express the following sentences in Italian you can feel confident that you have mastered the material in Chapter 10. The letter in brackets refers to a Parliamo exercise which you may find helpful.

1. Aren't you getting up now, Carla? (A) _____

2. I'm shaving later. (A) _____

3. Who's having a good time? (B) _____

4. Everyone is waking up. (B) _____

5. We're going to sleep in ten minutes. (C) _____

_____

6. He's not undressing because he doesn't want to undress! (D) _____

_____

7 Mrs. Collina, you have to get up today. (E) _____

_____

8. They hear me but they're not listening to me. (F) _____

_____

9. If you go, Michele, I'm going too. (G)_____

10. The train for Vicenza leaves from platform 9 at 9:20 p.m. (H)_____

_____

11. Who can read German? (I)_____

12. There she is, in the carriage with Dino. (J)_____

13. Gee, you're lazy, Elena! (K)_____

14. You haven't understood anything because you don't want to understand anything. (L)_____

_____

15. Of course I can drive a car but I can't go out now. (N)_____

_____

S. Componimento.

1. As secretary of your sporting club you're organising an outing to town for everyone who played in the team during the year. You now have to send out the notice to everyone (they only read Italian, of course) with the following details:

   What sort of outing.
   Where in town.
   How to get there by public transport. Include: times of departure and arrival; what stop to get on and off at.
   What they have to bring to eat and drink.
   Design your notice so that everyone will understand everything clearly:

   _____
   _____
   _____
   _____
   _____
   _____
   _____
   _____
   _____
   _____
   _____
   _____
   _____
   _____
   _____

2. **Keep an Italian diary for a week. Record what you did from the moment you got up to the time you went to bed:**

lunedì:_____

_____

_____

_____

martedì:_____

_____

_____

_____

mercoledì:_____

_____

_____

_____

giovedì:_____

_____

_____

_____

venerdì:_____

_____

_____

_____

sabato:_____

_____

_____

_____

domenica:_____

_____

_____

_____

_____

T. Non siamo ladroni.
Read the letter on page 144 of the textbook then answer the following questions in English:

1. Who did the students write to?_____

_____

2. Why did they write?_____

_____

3. How many days passed before they were able to write?_____

_____

_____

4. What reason did they give for their actions?_____

_____

_____

5. Who is Gianfranco and what do they say about him?_____

_____

_____

6. The students are trying to be funny when they say, ''Non siamo dei ladroni.'' Explain the poor attempt at a pun.

_____

_____

7. After reading the letter, the proprietor tells Gianfranco what he thinks about the students (and their pun too). Write, in Italian, what you think he might say:

_____

_____

_____

_____

_____

_____

_____

A. La posta e i telefoni.
The following questions relate to the Cultural Unit, La posta e i telefoni, on pages 140-141 of the textbook:

1. Explain to a non Italian speaking friend what a **distributore di francobolli** is and how to use it.

_____

_____

_____

2. Explain too, what he'll need to make a phone call and how he can obtain what he needs.

_____

_____

_____

3. Now he wants to ring Bari from Catania. How does he go about it?

_____

_____

_____

4. **Fabio is suspected by Interpol of belonging to an undercover organisation. You've been authorised to do a phone tap and now you have to report this conversation to headquarters. What did they say? (In other words, translate the conversation into English!!!) See page 141 of the textbook.**

☑ **Luisa:** ___Hello. Is that the Perugia Tennis Club?___

Fabio:_____

Luisa:_____

_____

_____

_____

_____

_____

_____

_____

_____

_____

_____

_____

_____

_____

B. Belluno.
Look carefully at this services map of the city of Belluno, then answer the questions related to it:

CITTÀ DI BELLUNO
Mappa dei servizi

■	Stadio
🏛	Cattedrale
⛸	Palaghiaccio
?	Ufficio informazioni
😃	Teatro Comunale
	Piscina
▬	Poste e telegrafi
◎	Palazzetto dello sport
📖	Centro Culturale
☎	Telefoni
	Carabinieri
🚆	Stazione ferroviaria
	Sala stampa
H	Ospedale
	Auditorium
	Ufficio Universiade
	Polizia
EPT	Ente Provinciale Turismo

1. Dov'è Belluno?_____

2. Dov'è la biblioteca?_____

3. Quali posti sono d'interesse per i turisti?_____
_____

4. Che cosa si può fare di giorno?_____
_____

5. Che cosa si può fare di sera?_____
_____

6. Quali posti preferisci visitare, tu?_____
_____

7. Dove preferisci non andare?_____
_____

8. Come si chiama il fiume che passa vicino Belluno?_____

C. Address this envelope to a high school teacher called Sandra Romani in Monza. She lives in Viale 20 Settembre flat 4B number 38. The post code is 20050. Note: The street number always follows the street name. The abbreviation of the provincial capital is written in brackets after the town name:

D. These drawings tell you how to use a telephone. Write the appropriate instruction under each drawing:
✆ fare il numero ✆ dire pronto ✆ alzare il ricevitore ✆ introdurre il gettone

1._____

2._____

3._____

4._____

E. Il Bancomat.

The following are excerpts from a brochure. There may be quite a few words you've never seen before, nevertheless try to understand as much as you can and answer the following questions:

Il Bancomat è semplice

Prelevare denaro contante dal tuo conto corrente tramite il BANCOMAT è molto semplice anche se non hai mai avuto modo di utilizzare apparecchiature elettroniche.

Lo Sportello Automatico può anche non essere della tua banca perché, come abbiamo già detto, con il BANCOMAT puoi utilizzare Sportelli Automatici anche di altre banche.

L'unica cosa che ti serve, oltre naturalmente al conto corrente, è la *carta* BANCOMAT.

Prelevare a qualunque ora, in qualunque località

1. What exactly is il **Bancomat**?_____

2. Do they say it is difficult to operate?_____

3. When and where can you use it?_____

_____

4. What is **lo sportello automatico**?_____

Now write a humorous caption for each drawing:

_____   _____   _____

_____   _____   _____

_____   _____   _____